# Hijama Therapy

## The Art and Science of

## Cupping

## (A Forgotten Sunnah)

By

**AfshanNaaz**

# Contents

# Chapter 1:
# Influence of Hijama in My Life

For centuries, ancient wisdom has recognized the body's innate capacity for healing. Hijama, also known as cupping therapy, is a therapeutic technique with deep roots in traditional medicine, masterfully makes use of this potential. This age-old practice involves creating suction on the skin to stimulate blood flow, promote detoxification, and alleviate a wide range of ailments.Amongst the pages of this book I have aimed to pen down my own experiences with hijama – the incredible benefits I gained and the transformative effects it had on my overall well-being. We will explore the profound benefits of hijama, from its historical and religious origins to its contemporary applications, uncovering the remarkable ways in which it can transform your life.

Cupping therapy, while gaining popularity today, is actually an ancient healing method. Its roots can be traced back to ancient Egypt, China, and the Middle East. One of the world's oldest medical books, the Ebers Papyrus, written around 1550 BC, talks about using cupping for fevers, pain, dizziness, women's health issues, and other problems.

The Egyptians shared this practice with the ancient Greeks, who used it to treat almost every illness. In traditional Chinese medicine, it's closely linked to acupuncture. The command of cupping is recommended in Islam as the sunnah of the Prophet Muhammad … the Messenger of Allah said,

*'Indeed, in cupping (hijama) there is healing.' (Muslim No. 4058).*

## Transormative Effects of Hijama on Health

During Covid19 world was engulfed in a collective anxiety as the pandemic spread. Everywhere you turned, there was fear, loss, uncertainty, new of people dying and loved ones passing away. Life turned more bleak and it was, without a doubt, the worst year of my life.

As a medical esthetician and a skincare formulator, I've spent my entire career working in hospitals and clinics, mostly in the Middle East. From Sharjah to Dubai, my experience in the medical field has always been in hospitals and clinics, positions that, while rare, gave me insight into the human body and its ailments.

One day, I woke up to find my right hand paralyzed. My fingers wouldn't move, and my hand felt dead. It was in that moment that I realized just how precious this one limb was, how connected it was to my entire body, my brain, and my sense of self. I was fortunate to be left-handed by birth, which allowed me to continue with most of my daily activities, but I'll never forget the fear and helplessness I felt when I opened my eyes and realized I couldn't move my right hand.

What followed was a series of doctor's visits. I was working at one of the best hospital in Dubai, so all my medical expenses were covered by insurance. I underwent X-rays, MRIs, and other scans. A barrage of medicines arrived at my home, and I was taking pills morning, noon, and night, all on a strict schedule. Despite all the tests and treatments, I was confused. The doctors diagnosed me with frozen shoulder, but the explanations didn't make much sense to me. I began to feel like just another case number, another patient whose treatment was being paid for by insurance, and I was growing more and more disillusioned.

A few days before all this, I had received my second dose of the COVID-19 vaccine. I couldn't help but wonder if this sudden paralysis was related to the vaccine or was something else entirely. But only God knows the truth. In the midst of my frustration and illness, I began to dig through my cupboards, and that's when I came across a book that had been gifted to me long ago: Healing with the Medicine of the Prophet (P.B.U.H) by Imam Ibn Qayyim al-Jawziyyah, edited by Abdul Rahman Abdullah. This book had been sitting in my cupboard for years, untouched, but something compelled me to open it then.

As I began to read the book, one particular verse on the 24th page caught my attention: *"Allah has not sent down a disease except that He also sent down its cure."*

Those words struck a chord deep within me. If every disease has a cure, then surely, I could find the cure for what I was experiencing. This idea began to take root in my mind, and I couldn't shake it off.

**A leap of Faith**

The next day, I had an appointment with an orthopedic surgeon. He discussed my condition in detail, explaining the problems with my shoulder—something about bones and muscles. He spoke for half an hour, but my mind couldn't focus. It was elsewhere, fixated on the verse I had read. It was as if that verse had lodged itself into my mind, drowning out everything else. The surgeon mentioned that the surgery would be covered by insurance, but all I could think about was how I would be allowing someone to cut into my body. That was the only thing that truly registered with me. When asked about scheduling the surgery, I could only say, "If Allah wants me to live with a non-functioning right hand, so be it. But I won't go under the knife."

I had made my stance clear —I was determined to heal myself, without surgery, and I would come back with a fully functional hand. This was the challenge I set for myself, driven by the confidence those verses had given me. But beneath that confidence, there was also fear. I had just rejected a world-renowned surgeon, believing I could heal myself. What if I failed? What if my condition worsened? These thoughts weighed on me, but the verses from the book had touched me deeply. They became my guiding light.

So, I decided to take a leap of faith and booked an appointment for Hijama. I was determined to find my cure without surgery, and Hijama was the path I chose – the one that had incredibly positive effect on not only my paralyze hand, but on my overall well-being.

**Positive Outcome**

Within six months, my hand, which had once been paralyzed, regained about 90% of its movement. This wasn't just the result of Hijama alone but also a combination of Hijama , moving cupping and exercise. While traditional massages do increase blood circulation, they press the skin downward. In contrast, moving cupping, which uses suction to pull the skin upwards, is more beneficial as it directs blood flow in a way that enhances the healing process.

The relief I felt after each Hijama session was profound. My body felt lighter, almost as if a burden had been lifted. The first session was challenging; I didn't feel much improvement, which later I understood as a healing crisis—a natural part of the body's response to this deep detoxification process. But as I continued, the benefits became more and more apparent, reinforcing my belief in the power of Hijama and the importance of continually honing my skills to help others experience the same healing.

Within eight months, I was able to move my hand again. I remember I couldn't help but go back to the doctor and his nurse to show that I had, in fact, cured my hand without any surgical processes.

**From Patient to Practitioner**

After experiencing the profound effects of Hijama on my own health, I felt compelled to learn more about this ancient healing practice. I enrolled in a diploma course in Hijama in India, which marked the beginning of my journey into this world of holistic healing. Once I completed my training, I started offering Hijama sessions to my family, friends and anyone came across my way with pain and had belief in holistic healing. I did it all for free, purely out of a desire to help others and practice what I had learned. I quickly found myself doing Hijama almost every day after my regular work hours, and I genuinely enjoyed it.

But my thirst for knowledge didn't stop there. I pursued another diploma course in Hijama from the UK because I wanted to perfect my skills. I knew there was always more to learn, especially about something that had such a significant impact on my life. Even now, I continue to seek out new learning opportunities. If a better course on Hijama comes along, I wouldn't hesitate to take it. For me, it's about constantly refining my knowledge and techniques, revisiting and brushing up on what I know to ensure I'm offering the best possible care to others.

A few months after I started practicing Hijama, I treated a group of young women, around 18 or 20 years old, who were dealing with polycystic ovary syndrome (PCOS). Their periods were irregular, and one of them hadn't had her period for three months. I performed a session of Hijama combined with moving cupping, and I also recommended some dietary changes. To my amazement, within two days, they called me to say their periods had started. These young women have since become regular clients, continuing to use Hijama to help manage their symptoms.

Every month, I made it a point to have Hijama performed on myself. I even visited almost all the Hijama clinics in the UAE to observe different techniques and approaches. The pain and struggle, which had lasted almost a year, taught me a profound lesson. Allah has gifted me with the knowledge of Hijama, and I truly believe it's something everyone should experience. But it's important to understand that the benefits of Hijama don't always come after just one session. The real healing happens over multiple sessions, and with each one, you feel better and better. Hijama not only cured my hand but also helped me think positively. It pulled me out of the depression and anxiety that had plagued me and helped me gave me a more positive mindset.

Even if you're on medication, Hijama can still be beneficial. You should never stop your medications abruptly; instead, continue with them while incorporating Hijama into your routine. For example, my thyroid levels have improved significantly over time, allowing me to gradually reduce my medication dosage. My prolactin levels, which were once high, have also decreased dramatically with consistent Hijama treatments.

### Hijama's Healing Crisis

Once your blood circulations increases and your body enters a healing crisis, many people get scared and stop the treatment. A healing crisis is just your body's way of detoxifying itself after Hijama. It's crucial not to stop at that point. You need to continue with more sessions to fully experience the healing effects. Over time, you'll notice a change—not just in your body, but in your entire outlook on life. You'll feel healthier, more positive, and gain clarity about what you need to do moving forward.

This was my personal experience, and it has shaped my belief in the power of Hijama.It's important to understand that Hijama isn't a one-time fix. For best results, it should be done regularly, tailored to your specific health needs. Even the healthiest person should consider doing Hijama at least three times a year. In today's world where we're constantly exposed to radiation s, Hijama can help detoxify your body and mind, making it a valuable practice for everyone.

## Hijama and Traditional Medicine

With modern allopathic medicine, the traditional methods of healing, despite effectively proven beneficial for centuries, takes a backseat. Which is why the renewed interest in hijama in modern times is indeed very interesting. Modern medicine acknowledges hijama therapy's efficacy in not only reducing pain and inflammation, enhancing blood circulation, and bolstering the immune system but also in treating a range of health conditions, including migraines, back pain, and arthritis.

Traditional (allopathic) medicine is based on modern scientific principles and practices. Its treatments and interventions are based on rigorous scientific research and clinical trials emphasizing precise diagnosis through advanced diagnostic tools and methods, followed by targeted treatments, often involving pharmaceuticals or surgical interventions.The medical field is highly specialized, with practitioners focusing on specific areas of medicine, allowing for in-depth expertise and targeted care.

Hijama, on the other hand, aims to restore balance in the body and ensure the free flow of energy and blood, eliminating any blockages that can lead to illness.Hijama enhances the body's natural detoxification processes, as it views the body as an interconnected system, emphasizing the importance of treating the root causes of ailments rather than just the symptoms. In this manner, this approach is rather holistic in nature.

Not surprisingly, their methodologies differ quiet significantly from one another too. Traditional medicine makes use of surgical interventions to remove, repair, or replace parts of the body affected by disease or injury, taking aid from advanced diagnostic tools such as MRI, CT scans, X-rays, blood tests, and genetic testing to accurately diagnose conditions. Furthermore, various therapies, including physical therapy, radiation therapy, and chemotherapy, are employed to treat and manage different conditions.

Traditional medicine employs the use of medications to treat, manage, or prevent diseases, while Hijama is a natural therapy that doesn't involve the use of pharmaceuticals or invasive procedures.It involves creating suction on the skin using cups, either by dry cuppingwhere cups are placed on the skin, creating suction without making incisions. The other method is wet cupping where  small incisions are made on the skin to draw out a small amount of blood. These processes will be discussed in great detail in the following chapter. By drawing out toxins and impurities, hijama supports the body's natural detoxification processes.

This is by no means to say that traditional or Western

medicine should be disregarded completely. Rather, combining the strengths of hijama and traditional medicine can offer a more holistic approach to health and wellness.

## Holistic Healing

Holistic healing is an approach to health care that considers the whole person – body, mind, and spirit – rather than just treating specific symptoms or illnesses. Hijamafits perfectly into the holistic health paradigm and can be a valuable component of a holistic lifestyle, complementing other natural therapies and healthy habits.Hijama and traditional medicine each have their unique strengths and limitations. Integrating these approaches can lead to a more holistic, patient-centered, and effective health care experience.

Here's how they can complement each other:

### 1. Complementary Therapies:

Hijama can be used alongside traditional treatments to enhance overall well-being. Consider combining hijama with other holistic therapies such as acupuncture, herbal medicine, and massage therapy to enhance overall health and well-being.

### 2. Adopt a Healthy Diet:

Support your body's natural healing processes with a nutritious diet rich in whole foods, fruits, vegetables, lean proteins, and healthy fats. Avoid processed foods and excessive sugar, which can contribute to inflammation and toxin buildup.

### 3. Preventive Care:

Hijama's focus on detoxification and improved circulation can support preventive health measures, potentially reducing the need for more invasive treatments.

The Prophet Muhammad (peace be upon him) strongly advocated for hijama, asserting its efficacy in treating various ailments, excluding death. Divine guidance received during his ascension to the heavens further emphasized the importance of this practice.

I have found Hijama to be a powerful and natural therapy that aligns perfectly with the principles of holistic healing. By promoting balance, detoxification, pain relief, immune function, and mental well-being, hijama offers a comprehensive approach to health and wellness. From specific health issues to overall well-being, I have found Hijama to be an incredibly powerful remedy which not only cures, but also prevents any illnesses that may potentially occur in the future.

# Chapter 2:

# Hijama& types of cupping therapy.

This chapter explores different types of cupping, their methods, and their specific benefits. Understanding the variations in cupping can help practitioners and patients alike choose the most appropriate technique for their needs. Cupping encompasses various techniques that differ in their methods, intensity, and intended outcomes. From traditional cupping to modern adaptations, each method offers unique therapeutic benefits and is tailored to address specific health conditions.

### 1. Wet Cupping (Hijama)

Wet cupping, also known as Hijama, is a therapeutic technique based on creating suction on the skin's surface to draw out blood, which may carry toxins, pathogens, or bad humors. This method is considered a form of detoxification and is often used to treat a range of physical and spiritual ailments. To understand Hijama, it's important to consider both the physiological processes involved and the traditional beliefs that underpin the practice.

### Endorsement by the Prophet (P.B.U.H)

The Prophet of Allah (P.B.U.H) stressed upon Hijama on several occasions, emphasizing its significance in the treatment of various ailments.

**Process of Hijama**

The first step involves creating a vacuum within a cup, which is then applied to the skin. The suction causes the skin and underlying tissues to be pulled into the cup, increasing localized blood flow.

After the initial dry cupping stage, small superficial incisions are made on the skin. This step allows the release of blood, believed to carry toxins.

Reapplying the cups over these incisions creates a gentle suction that draws out a small quantity of blood. The cups are then removed, and the area is cleansed and bandaged.

**Benefits of Wet Cupping (Hijama)**

Despite its long history, Hijama has gained renewed popularity in recent years due to its numerous physical health benefits. Here are some of the ways Hijama can enhance your overall well-being:

**Boosts Circulation and Blood Flow**: The suction created by the cups draws blood to the skin's surface, increasing blood flow to the affected areas. This improved circulation ensures that oxygen and essential nutrients are delivered more efficiently to tissues and organs, promoting faster healing and better overall health.

**Detoxifies the Body**: Hijama is known for its detoxification properties. By drawing out stagnant blood and toxins, it supports the liver and kidneys in their natural detoxification processes, cleansing the body from the inside out.

**Relieves Pain and Inflammation:** Hijama is effective for chronic pain and inflammation, especially conditions like arthritis, back pain, and muscle soreness. The therapy reduces inflammation and alleviates pain, providing much-needed relief.

**Supports Immune Function**: By stimulating the body's natural defense mechanisms, Hijama helps to enhance immune responses. Regular sessions can contribute to a stronger immune system.

**Aids in Digestion**: Hijama improves digestive health by promoting better circulation and reducing inflammation in the digestive tract. It aids in reducing bloating and relieving common gastrointestinal problems.

**Enhances Skin Health:** The detoxification effects of Hijama can improve skin conditions like acne, eczema, and psoriasis. The therapy promotes youthful skin by increasing collagen production and improving elasticity.

**Improves Respiratory Health**

For individuals with asthma, bronchitis, or allergies, Hijama can help by reducing congestion, improving lung function, and enhancing respiratory health.

**Supports Athletic Performance and Recovery:**

Athletes benefit from Hijama through improved circulation, reduced muscle tension, and faster recovery from injuries.

**Balances Energy Levels:** Hijama is believed to remove blockages in the body's energy flow, promoting better vitality and mental clarity. Those who practice Hijama regularly report feeling more energized and balanced.

**Islamic Guidelines and Sunnah**

The Prophet (P.B.U.H) advised his followers to treat the sick with sadaqah. It is recommended that those undergoing Hijama give sadaqah afterward and offer two rak'aat of nafl, asking Allah for recovery and thanking Him for the ability to follow the Sunnah.

**Warnings and Precautions**

**Disposal of Cups:** Cups used for one person must not be reused on another to prevent the transmission of diseases such as Hepatitis B, Hepatitis C, and HIV/AIDS.

**Types of Instruments:** Various instruments are available for cupping today. While plastic cups are commonly used, care must be taken not to reuse them. Avoid using glass cups or balloons inside cups, as viruses can penetrate these materials.

**Sanitization of Cups:** No amount of boiling can disinfect cups from certain viruses, especially Hepatitis. Strict hygiene protocols must be followed.

**Common Applications:**

Hijama is often employed to address chronic pain conditions, improve blood circulation, and facilitate detoxification. Additionally, it is utilized as a treatment for specific ailments such as migraines and various skin disorders.

**2.Dry Cupping**

Dry cupping, the most prevalent form of cupping therapy, involves creating a vacuum within cups placed on the skin without breaching the skin's layers. This technique focuses on elevating the skin, underlying tissues, and muscles to enhance blood flow and facilitate healing processes.

Once suction is achieved, the skin and superficial muscle tissue are drawn into the cup. This suction causes the skin to expand, increasing the space between the skin and the underlying muscles, fascia, and blood vessels. The mechanical lifting of the skin and tissues leads to several physiological responses that contribute to the therapeutic effects of dry cupping.

**Benefits:**

Dry cupping is especially beneficial in augmenting

circulation, delivering oxygenated blood to the treated area, alleviates muscle tension and discomfort. It also ameliorates respiratory issues by expanding the airways. Dry cupping also promotes lymphatic drainage, which is crucial for detoxification and immune function. This detoxifying effect is one reason why dry cupping is often recommended for conditions involving inflammation, chronic pain, and general fatigue.

**Common Applications:**

It is commonly applied to areas subjected to muscular pain, stiffness, and sports-related injuries. It is also used to treat chronic pain conditions, such as fibromyalgia.

### 3. Fire Cupping

The defining characteristic of fire cupping is the use of fire to create suction. The process begins with the practitioner lighting a cotton ball soaked in alcohol or another flammable substance. The burning cotton ball is then briefly placed inside a glass cup, heating the air inside. The cup is quickly placed on the patient's skin, and as the hot air cools, it contracts, creating a vacuum. This vacuum pulls the skin and underlying tissues upward into the cup, generating the characteristic suction of cupping therapy. The cups typically remain in place for 5 to 15 minutes.

This method of suction creation through fire has several unique effects:

## 4. Rapid Vacuum Formation:

The use of heat allows for the quick creation of a strong vacuum, ensuring that the suction is immediate and effective. This strong suction can penetrate deeper layers of tissue compared to other cupping methods.

### *Thermal Effect:*

The residual warmth from the fire remains in the cup for a short time, providing a gentle heating effect to the skin and underlying tissues. This heat can help relax muscles, reduce stiffness, and enhance the overall therapeutic effect.

### Benefits:

Fire cupping is particularly effective for relaxing tight muscles and releasing fascial adhesions. The combined effects of heat and suction work together to stretch and loosen the fascia—a connective tissue that surrounds muscles and organs. It can also help clear congestion in the respiratory system. Moreover, it provides a soothing, warming sensation beneficial for conditions like arthritis.

### Common Applications:

Fire cupping is commonly employed for deep tissue relaxation and addressing respiratory conditions such as asthma and bronchitis. It also provides relief from cold symptoms and is beneficial in treating arthritis and other ailments characterized by cold and dampness in the body.

## 5. Moving Cupping (Massage Cupping)

Moving cupping, also known as massage cupping, merges the advantages of cupping and massage therapy. It involves the dynamic application of cups, rather than static placement, to treat larger body areas and improve overall circulation and muscle tone.

Oil or lotion is applied to the skin to facilitate smooth cup movement. Cups are affixed to the skin with suction and then maneuvered across the skin in a gliding motion. The direction of movement can vary depending on the targeted area and desired outcome. This technique typically lasts for approximately 15 to 30 minutes.

### Benefits:

By moving the cups across the skin, massage cupping can improve overall microcirculation in the area, which is crucial for maintaining healthy tissue function and accelerating the healing process. It stimulates blood flow and lymphatic drainage, effectively releasing muscle knots and tension across a broader area. Additionally, it can enhance the absorption of medicinal oils or lotions applied during the therapy.

Furthermore, the mechanical stimulation of the skin and tissues during massage cupping can interfere with the transmission of pain signals to the brain, a phenomenon known as the "gate control theory" of pain. By activating mechanoreceptors (sensory receptors that respond to mechanical pressure), massage cupping can reduce the intensity of pain signals and provide relief from chronic pain conditions.

**Common Applications:**

Moving cupping is commonly applied to alleviate back and neck pain, reduce generalized muscle stiffness, enhance skin tone and texture, and treat cellulite while improving lymphatic drainage.

### 6. Flash Cupping

Flash cupping is a technique that involves rapid, repetitive application and removal of cups. This method is less intense than other cupping forms and is often employed for sensitive patients or individuals requiring blood flow stimulation without the intensity of prolonged cupping sessions.

Cups are applied to the skin and swiftly removed after creating suction. This process is repeated multiple times within a specific area. The rapid application and removal of the cups generate a gentle, rhythmic suction on the skin.

**Benefits:**

Flash cupping stimulates blood flow without the prolonged suction associated with other methods, reducing the risk of bruising.

It is suitable for sensitive areas or individuals with low tolerance for more intense cupping techniques. Additionally, it can serve as a preparatory step before other cupping modalities and promotes relaxation while improving overall circulation.

**Common Applications:**

Flash cupping is commonly applied to sensitive or painful areas where longer cupping might be overly intense. It can also be used as a preparatory step before other cupping modalities. Additionally, it promotes relaxation and mild stimulation of blood flow, making it suitable for areas with delicate skin or underlying structures.

### 7. Water Cupping

Water cupping, although less common, involves the use of warm water within the cups to generate suction. This method combines the benefits of hydrotherapy with traditional cupping.

The cups are filled with warm water. The cups are then applied to the skin, and the water aids in creating a gentle suction. The warmth of the water provides an additional soothing effect to the cupping therapy.

**Benefits:**

Water cupping is gentle on the skin, making it suitable for sensitive individuals. The warmth from the water helps relax muscles and improve circulation. This method effectively combines the benefits of cupping with those of hydrotherapy while reducing the risk of skin irritation or bruising.

**Common Applications:**

Water cupping is commonly used on sensitive skin areas and for patients with low tolerance for traditional cupping methods. It provides general relaxation and mild muscle tension relief while enhancing the effects of hydrotherapy treatments.

Cupping therapy offers a wide range of methods, each with its own specific benefits and applications. Whether you are seeking to relieve muscle pain, detoxify your body, or enhance your overall well-being, there is likely a type of cupping that can suit your needs. Understanding the differences between these methods is crucial for both practitioners and patients to ensure the most effective and appropriate treatment. As with any therapy, it's important to consult with a qualified professional to determine which type of cupping is best for your specific condition and health goals.

# Chapter 3:

# History of Cupping therapy

Cupping is among the oldest natural healing methods known to humankind. Archaeological findings suggest that this practice dates back as far as 3000 B.C. Spanning millennia and diverse cultures, this ancient technique has been employed for its potential healing benefits. This chapter takes you back through time to explore the evolution of Hijama, from its origins in ancient civilizations to its contemporary resurgence. By examining the historical context, practitioners, and cultural influences, I aim to illuminate the enduring appeal and significance of this therapeutic modality.

The earliest documented evidence of cupping dates back to around 1550 B.C. in Egypt. Found within the Ebers Papyrus—one of the world's oldest medical textbooks—references to cupping as a treatment emerged. Papyrus was a common writing material in ancient Egpyt and the Mediterranean, created from the pithy stem of a water plant, making this document a significant historical artifact.

In ancient Egypt, cupping was believed to restore balance within the body and was often employed alongside other traditional therapies, such as herbal medicine and bloodletting. The practice was thought to remove harmful substances from the body and improve the flow of life energy, known as ka in Egyptian belief.

Ancient Greece, a cradle of Western civilization, also witnessed the practice of cupping as a therapeutic treatment. The renowned physician Hippocrates, often hailed as the "Father of Medicine," extensively employed cupping for treating a wide array of ailments. His comprehensive approach to healthcare included cupping as a pivotal component. Hippocrates believed that cupping could effectively address both internal diseases and structural problems. His writings offer insights into the application of cupping for conditions such as angina, menstrual irregularities, and other disorders. The Greek physician Galen was instrumental in popularizing cupping as a medical treatment. He highlighted its ability to improve blood circulation and cure ailments. Galen's endorsement significantly expanded the practice of cupping across Europe and the Islamic world.

While the exact techniques and specific conditions treated might have varied among Greek practitioners, the foundational principles of cupping—creating a vacuum to draw blood to the surface—remained consistent. It's plausible that the Greeks, like other ancient cultures, combined cupping with other therapeutic methods to achieve optimal results.

In the East, bloodletting and wet cupping have been fundamental components of medical traditions for centuries and continue to be practiced today.China has made substantial contributions to the evolution of cupping therapy. Anthropological findings have indicated that cupping practices existed in China as early as 1,000 BC. Its history can be traced back to the Han Dynasty (206 BC – 220 AD), where it was initially documented. The Yellow Emperor's Classic of Internal Medicine, an ancient text dating back to around 300 BC, further expanded on these early practices. Traditional Chinese Medicine views cupping as a method to invigorate the flow of vital energy, known as qi (chi), and enhance blood circulation.

Chinese cupping is a rich history deeply intertwined with healing and innovation. The Chinese expanded the use of the cupping technique to surgery, which was called wet cupping. As an ancient Taoist medical practice, it was prevalent in Imperial Chinese courts as well. Its earliest documented use can be attributed to Ge Hong, who detailed it in his renowned work, the "Handbook of Prescriptions for Emergencies."

Throughout Chinese history, cupping has evolved in technique and application, but it has always remained a key component of TCM, valued for its therapeutic and preventive benefits. Today, it is still practiced globally, often combined with modern medical practices.

The practice of cupping persisted through the centuries and

was integrated into Islamic medicine during the Islamic Golden Age – an age which witnessed remarkable medical progress, and cupping therapy flourished under the expertise of scholars like Ibn Sina, Al-Zahrawi, and Al-Razi. Building upon the knowledge inherited from previous cultures, these luminaries significantly advanced cupping practices within the comprehensive field of Islamic medicine.

Cupping became a part of the Arab Muslim community's practices owing to the cultural interactions with the Greeks and Romans, principally through Alexandria and Byzantium. The Prophet Muhammad (PBUH) significantly enhanced the status of cupping, transforming it from a simple medical treatment to a fundamental aspect of both physical and spiritual health within Islamic society. His support for cupping extended beyond its physical and mental benefits, ascribing to it deep spiritual significance. By associating cupping with purity and spiritual connection, the Prophet elevated its standing to an unprecedented level of esteem.

This endorsement by the Prophet (PBUH) profoundly influenced the subsequent incorporation of cupping into Islamic medical practices and cultural traditions. It cultivated a profound belief in cupping's ability to heal not only the body but also the soul. As a result, cupping became an indispensable component of Islamic healthcare, revered by both practitioners and patients due to its association with the Prophet's teachings.

In Indonesia, the beginning of cupping is strongly believed to be introduced by Gujarati and Arab traders who brought Islam to the archipelago around the 12th century. Supporting this theory, several individuals with Middle Eastern heritage reported having been familiar with cupping since their childhood. The popularity of cupping in Indonesia surged in the 1990s, primarily due to Indonesians returning from studies or work in Malaysia, India, and the Middle East. During the 20th century, the practice underwent a transformation with the introduction of thick, shatterproof glass cups, leading to advancements in cupping techniques.

Cupping technique soon spread through the medicine world, throughout Asian and European civilizations. Each country has their own name for cupping therapy as well as their own methods of cupping. Here are some of the names that cupping is referred to in other cultures; Hijamah / Hijama / Baguanfa / jiaofa, / Bentusa, / Vendouse, Gac Hoi /, Bahnkes, Kyukaku, / Ventosaterapia, / SchrÖpftherapie, / Kupa Cekme, / Jiaofa,/ Bankovani, / Ventouzzes, and Vacuume Terapi.

Cupping became widespread across Europe between the 14th and 17th centuries, particularly flourishing during the Renaissance. In Italy, it was the favored treatment for arthritis and gout. Throughout the 18th century, the majority of European physicians employed cupping for ailments such as the common cold and chest infections. Records show that renowned surgeons, such as

Paracelsus, Ambroise Pare, Pierre Dionis, and Charles Kennedy, utilized cupping as a therapeutic treatment. These medical pioneers recognized and documented the positive impact of cupping on human health.

However, the emergence of evidence-based medicine towards the end of the 18th century led to a decline in the popularity of cupping. The improper practice of bloodletting resulted in a substantial increase in fatalities, leading to its widespread condemnation within the medical community. Consequently, the emerging scientific model of medicine began discrediting not only bloodletting but also other established traditional therapies in its pursuit of medical authority.

## The Evolution of Instruments for Cupping

Historical documents provide evidence of the use of specific tools and vessels for cupping as a therapeutic treatment during this ancient period. Ancient texts tell us that hollow animal horns were used to create a vacuum, which helped draw out toxins and treat illnesses like bites, stings, infections, and other diseases. To use the horn, the pointed end was placed on the skin, and the air inside was sucked out by mouth through a small hole, creating a vacuum. Once the vacuum was formed, the hole was quickly sealed with a piece of dried grass, held in place by the healer's tongue. Another method involved burning dry leaves or paper inside the horn to create suction, which was maintained until the heat dissipated.

Different cultures used various materials for cupping vessels. Along the west coast of North America, such as Vancouver Island, sea shells were used. In Europe, Asia, Africa, and North America, animal horns, like those from buffalo, were commonly used. In the Kelantanese Malays, buffalo horns were particularly popular.

In the 19th century, European medical practitioners commonly employed leeches for bloodletting. France's extensive use of this practice is evident in its reported import of approximately 40 million leeches for this purpose.

The tradition of bloodletting in Finland dates back to at least the 15th century and persists in some sauna settings. Cow horn cups were traditionally utilized for this practice.

Over time, cupping evolved, and bamboo cups replaced animal horns in some regions, especially in China. Bamboo cups were heated by immersing them in boiling water, and the heated cups were placed on specific points of the body. The temperature difference created a vacuum, which caused suction on the skin. Healers would leave the bamboo cups on the skin for about 10 minutes, reheating them as needed to continue the treatment. Eventually, cupping vessels changed and were replaced by materials like glass, plastic, and rubber, though bamboo cups are still used in some places today.

## Resurgence in Contemporary Times

In the 21st century, hijama, or cupping therapy, has experienced a significant resurgence. While this ancient practice has been a foundation of traditional medicine for centuries, the modern world has seen a renewed interest in its benefits. Cupping has emerged as a prominent example, gaining wider acceptance within the medical community. People are increasingly seeking drug-free, gentle, and relaxing treatments as well as the widespread sharing of information through social media and other digital platforms, leading to a surge in popularity for cupping.

The rediscovery of hijama has been fueled by a combination of factors, including an increased awareness of the limitations of conventional medicine and a growing interest in traditional healing methods. People are turning to hijama as a complementary therapy, seeking relief from chronic pain, stress, and other ailments. This resurgence has been particularly strong in communities with a historical connection to the practice, but it has also spread to new regions, where people are exploring it as part of a broader wellness trend.

The modern revival of hijama has also been boosted by endorsements from celebrities and athletes who have publicly embraced cupping therapy. Perhaps one of the most notable moments in recent history was during the 2016 Summer Olympics, when American swimmer Michael Phelps was seen with circular bruises on his back—marks left by cupping therapy. Phelps credited hijama with helping him recover faster between competitions, and his visible use of the therapy brought widespread attention to the practice.

Other famous figures who have turned to cupping include actress Gwyneth Paltrow, who has long been an advocate for various holistic treatments, and basketball star LeBron James, who uses cupping as part of his recovery regimen, and celebrities like Victoria Beckham and  Denise Richards have publicly embraced cupping, sharing photos of the temporary marks it leaves. Athletes such as Olympic swimmers Wang Qun and Stephanie Rice have also adopted the practice, hoping for performance benefits. These high-profile endorsements have helped demystify hijama and have encouraged more people to explore its benefits.

As hijama has reemerged in contemporary times, it has found a place within the broader field of modern holistic medicine. Practitioners of holistic health often emphasize the importance of treating the whole person—mind, body, and spirit—rather than just focusing on symptoms. Hijama aligns well with this philosophy, as it is believed to help balance the body's energy, improve circulation, and remove toxins, contributing to overall well-being.

# Hijama Therapy

In modern holistic practices, hijama is often used alongside other therapies such as acupuncture, massage, and herbal medicine. This integration has allowed hijama to be more widely accepted and practiced, even in regions where it was not traditionally known. It has also led to an increase in certified practitioners who combine traditional techniques with modern knowledge, ensuring that patients receive safe and effective treatments.

As a result, cupping therapy has become more mainstream, with many wellness centers and holistic health practitioners offering it as part of their services. This modern embrace of hijama reflects a broader trend of blending ancient practices with contemporary health and wellness strategies, ensuring that this traditional therapy continues to thrive in today's world.

# Chapter 4:
# Sunnah and Religious Aspect of Hijama

### Psychophysical therapy and Tibb-e-Nabawi (Medicine of the Prophet)

Psycho-Physical Therapy (PPT) is an integrative therapeutic approach that places central importance on the body's active engagement in the healing process. By merging psychological and physical therapeutic techniques, PPT offers a simultaneous treatment of mind and body.

Psychophysical therapy recognizes the intricate connection between the mind and body. By addressing both psychological and physical aspects of health, it offers a comprehensive approach to well-being. This therapeutic modality is crucial for conditions that manifest both mentally and physically, such as chronic pain, anxiety disorders, and eating disorders. Interestingly, this holistic perspective aligns with the core principles of Islamic spiritual treatments.

Islam offers a parallel approach known as Islamic Spiritual Therapy, which is rooted in Quranic principles and the Sunnah (the Prophet Muhammad (PBUH)'s teachings and practices). This therapeutic modality focuses on healing psychological ailments through spiritual means. Often referred to as Tibb-e-Nabawi, or Prophetic Medicine, it emphasizes the curative aspects of the Prophet's guidance. Cupping therapy is one example of a treatment within this framework.

Al-Bukhari narrates that:

"there is cure in three substances, a drink of honey, a slash with a knife used for cupping, and cauterizing by fire. I forbid my Nation (Ummah) from cauterizing by fire."

**Religious Significance of Hijama in Islam**

Hijama is regarded as an act of Sunnah because it was practiced and recommended by the Prophet Muhammad (PBUH) himself. The significance of Hijama in Islam is highlighted through various Hadiths—records of the sayings and actions of the Prophet. For example, in Sahih Bukhari, one of the most trusted collections of Hadith, the Prophet is reported to have said, "The best treatment you can use is cupping." This statement emphasizes the importance the Prophet placed on this form of therapy.

Furhtermore. importance of Hijama in the divine guidance can further be stressed by the following words which were related to the Prophet SAW on the night of Israa (ascension to the heaven) by angles: "O Mohammed, order your ummah (people) with Hijama (cupping)".– Saheeh, Sunan Tirmidhi.

## Importance of Hijama in Sunnah

Ibn al-Qaiyum (may Allah have mercy on him) mentions that the Messenger ﷺ was cupped on his head when he was afflicted with magic and that it is from the best of cures for this if performed correctly. [Zaad al Ma'aad (4/125-126)]

The practice of Hijama is supported by a number of Hadiths by the Prophet (PBUH) that describe its use for a wide range of ailments, from headaches to general fatigue. These references provide a religious foundation to incorporate Hijama into health practices, rendering it as both a remedy and a form of devotion.

Apart from headaches and general health benefits discussed in great detail in the previous chapters, the Prophet (PBUH) has specifically recommended Hijama for various ailments.

- Injuries:

  The Prophet experienced relief from bruising through Hijama.

Jaabir ibn Abdullaah (RA) reported that the Prophet (PBUH) fell from his horse onto the trunk of a palm tree and dislocated his foot. Waki' (RA) said, "Meaning the Prophet (PBUH) was cupped on (his foot) for bruising." [Saheeh Sunan ibn Maajah (2807)].

- Headaches:

Salma (RA), the servant of the Rasul (SAW) said, "Whenever someone would complain of a headache to the Rasul of Allaah (SAW), he (SAW) would advise them to perform Hijamah." [Saheeh Sunan abi Dawud (3858)].

- Sihr (Black Magic):

The Prophet underwent Hijama as a treatment for black magic, which is considered highly effective when performed correctly.

Ibn al-Qaiyum (RA) mentions that the Prophet (PBUH) was cupped on his head when he was afflicted with sihr and that it is from the best of cures for this if performed correctly. [Zaad al Ma'aad (4/125-126)].

- Poison:

The Prophet sought relief from poison through Hijama.

Abdullaah ibn Abbas (RA) reported that a Jewish woman gave poisoned meat to the Prophet (PBUH) so he (PBUH) sent her a message saying, "What caused you to do that?" She replied, "If you really are a Nabi then Allah will inform you of it and if you are not then I would save the people from you!" When the Prophet (PBUH) felt pain from it, he (PBUH) performed Hijama. Once he travelled while in Ihram and felt that pain and hence performed hijama. [Ahmed (1/305) the Hadeeth is Hasan].

The importance of Hijama, as clear through various incidences, in the Sunnah extends beyond its physical benefits. It has numerous spiritual benefits and rids you of ailment both of body and soul, if the procedure is done as per the teachings of the Prophet (PBUH), who has given a comprehensive detail about the procedure of hijama – from the benefits of hijama in during illness and strength, the time in accordance with the lunar calendar when it should be performed, the amount of blood that should be removed, the specific areas on the body where it yields the most benefit, and more general precautions, all of which shall be discussed in depth in the following chapters.

For an example, Ibn 'Umar (radiyallāhu 'anhumā) said: "O Nafi', the blood is boiling in me, find me a cupper, but let it be someone gentle if you can, not an old man or a young boy, for I heard the Messenger of Allah (salallāhu 'alaihi wasallam) say: 'Cupping on an empty stomach is better, and in it, there is healing and blessing, and it increases one's intellect and memory.

Hijama, for Muslims, is also as an act of faith and a way to gain spiritual reward. Following the Sunnah of the Prophet Muhammad (PBUH) one earns the pleasure of Allah. By engaging in practices that the Prophet endorsed, such as Hijama, Muslims fulfil a religious duty and align themselves with the teachings of Islam.

Hijama is also mentioned in connection with spiritual cleansing. Islamic scholars emphasize the practice as not only removing physical impurities from the body but also as a way to cleanse the soul. Islamic healing addresses the interconnectedness of mind, body, and soul. While Hijama cupping therapy is a minor medical procedure with immediate physical benefits, its impact extends beyond the physical realm. By inducing relaxation and alleviating anxiety and depression, Hijama contributes to overall well-being. Moreover, hijama is believed to be efficient in addressing spiritual and metaphysical issues.

Hijama is more than just a therapeutic practice in Islam; it is a revered Sunnah that carries deep religious significance. By following this practice, Muslims not only seek physical healing but also fulfill a spiritual obligation, reflecting the holistic approach to health and well-being that is central to Islamic teachings.

## Spiritual Benefits of Hijama in Islam

In Islam, the concept of health extends beyond the mere absence of illness. It encompasses a holistic approach that integrates physical, mental, and spiritual well-being. Hijama, as a Sunnah practice, is seen not only as a method of physical healing but also as a means to enhance spiritual well-being.

The Islamic perspective on health emphasizes the profound connection between physical and spiritual states. Hijama serves as a practical demonstration of this interconnectedness, illustrating how physical practices can influence spiritual well-being.

- The Concept of Barakah (Blessing):

In Islam, barakah refers to the divine blessings that enrich and enhance one's life. The practice of hijama is believed to carry barakah, as it is a Sunnah endorsed by the Prophet Muhammad (PBUH). By participating in this practice, Muslims seek not only physical healing but also spiritual blessings. The belief in barakah reinforces the idea that physical health improvements through hijama contribute to an overall sense of spiritual fulfillment.

- **The Role of Intentions (Niyyah):**

In Islam, the intention behind any action plays a crucial role in its spiritual significance. For hijama, the intention to follow the Sunnah of the Prophet (PBUH) and seek Allah's pleasure transforms a physical procedure into an act of worship. This connection between intention and action underscores the idea that physical health practices, when performed with sincere intentions, can lead to spiritual rewards and growth.

- **The Integration of Physical and Spiritual Health:**

Islamic teachings highlight that physical health is not

separate from spiritual well-being. The Prophet Muhammad (PBUH) emphasized the importance of maintaining good health as part of one's faith. Hijama, as a method of physical healing, aligns with this teaching by addressing physical ailments and promoting overall well-being. The practice reinforces the idea that caring for the body is an integral part of caring for the soul.

- **The Impact of Physical Health on Spiritual Practices:**

Physical health can influence one's ability to engage in spiritual practices. Good health enables individuals to perform their religious duties more effectively, such as prayer and fasting. By improving physical health through hijama, Muslims may find that they are better able to fulfill their spiritual obligations and engage in worship with greater devotion.

- **Spiritual Lessons from Physical Healing:**

The process of hijama itself can impart spiritual lessons. The act of removing toxins from the body can be seen as a metaphor for removing negative influences from one's life. This symbolic cleansing aligns with Islamic teachings on repentance and purification, reinforcing the connection between physical actions and spiritual growth.

Hijama, or cupping therapy, is more than just a physical

healing practice in Islam; it carries significant spiritual benefits. By following the Sunnah of the Prophet Muhammad (PBUH), Muslims enhance their spiritual well-being and fulfill a religious duty. The connection between physical and spiritual health is a central theme in Islamic teachings, and hijama exemplifies this integration.

The practice of hijama not only addresses physical ailments but also promotes spiritual cleansing, mindfulness, and overall well-being. Through this holistic approach, Muslims seek to balance their physical and spiritual states, aligning with Islamic principles of health and devotion. By embracing hijama, individuals contribute to their spiritual growth and strengthen their connection with Allah, embodying the Islamic understanding of holistic health and well-being.

**Incorporating Faith into Hijama Sessions**

**The Concept of Life-Energy and Its Implications**

Many spiritual traditions converge on the notion of a vital life force animating living beings. This energy, known as 'ki' in Japanese, 'chi' in Chinese, 'prana' in Indian, and 'ruḥ al-imān' (spirit of belief) in Sufi Islamic thought, is believed to circulate through the body along specific pathways. Disruptions to this energy flow are often associated with illness or imbalance.

Practices such as Hijama aim to harmonize and balance this life force. Proper breathing, as emphasized in Pranayama and certain

Sufi practices, is considered crucial for its cultivation. The concept of 'laṭā'if' in Sufism aligns with the idea of energy centers, similar to chakras in other traditions. Even the late Wilhelm Reich proposed the existence of a biological energy, 'orgone,' which he connected to proper breathing and overall well-being. Traditional Chinese Medicine (TCM) further links this life energy to blood circulation. The belief that blood carries 'qi' underscores the intricate relationship between physical and energetic health.

The concept of 'jinn' in Islamic belief adds another dimension to this understanding. While the symptoms, often linked to possession, and other times to mental illness (scientifically), it highlights the idea of external forces influencing the body's energy field. Symptoms associated with possession, such as nightmares, tingling sensations, and aversion to Quranic recitation, suggest disruptions to the body's energy balance.

This interdisciplinary perspective reveals a common thread across diverse cultures and spiritual traditions: the recognition of a vital life force and its influence on health and well-being. Based on available evidence, Hijama shares similarities with energy medicine, particularly acupuncture. Both practices aim to restore balance by addressing energy flow within the body. However, Hijama distinguishes itself by incorporating bloodletting, which is believed to detoxify the system.

By targeting and making small incisions on specific points on the body, Hijama is unclogs energy channels, promoting optimal flow. In addition to its physical benefits, Hijama has been employed to address spiritual imbalances associated with possession and black magic. The practice of reciting the Quran during sessions is rooted in the belief that it can expel harmful entities. While the concept of energy and spiritual influences on health is a complex one, the integration of Hijama within this framework offers a unique approach to holistic well-being.

**The Role of Faith in Healing**

As enunciated above, faith plays a crucial role in the healing process. It provides individuals with hope, resilience, and a sense of purpose.

In the context of Hijama, faith can strengthen the mind-body connection. A strong belief in the efficacy of Hijama can positively influence the body's response to treatment. Having faith in a treatment that is deemed well and beneficial to you by the God and endorsed and practiced by His Prophet (PBUH) enhances the healing process. Moreover, faith can accelerate recovery by promoting optimism and reducing stress.

Engaging in spiritual practices during and after hijama can offer solace and peace of mind. Being mindful of the spiritual healing aspect of hijama, or any treatment for that matter, is a very necessary element. And in order to ensure active mindfulness during and before hijama sessions, practitioners can consider the following:

**Prayer and supplication:**

Guiding patients in offering prayers and supplications before, during, and after the session can foster a deeper connection with Allah.

**Sharing relevant Quranic verses:**

Reciting or discussing Quranic verses related to healing and well-being can provide spiritual inspiration.

**Emphasizing the Sunnah:**

Explaining the Prophet Muhammad (PBUH)'s recommendations for Hijama can reinforce its significance within Islamic tradition.

**The role of Hajjam:**

The therapists who perform the hijama, called Hajjam, play a vital role in creating a spiritually enriching environment as well. A therapist's personal faith can influence their ability to create a spiritually conducive and healing atmosphere where the patient can feel relaxed and benefits properly from the sessions. Offering gentle guidance on Islamic practices related to healing can be beneficial. But it should also be kept in mind that while incorporating faith, it is essential to maintain professional boundaries and ethics. It is crucial to honor the patient's faith and beliefs, avoiding any imposition of personal views, regardless of their faith, religion or any other bias that mind come in way of this healing journey and cause any obstruction.

# Chapter 5:
# Best Days for Hijama

Specific days are considered better for performing Hijama based on the teachings of Prophet Muhammad (PBUH). The Prophet highly recommended cupping therapy and outlined days in the lunar month when it would be most effective. According to several Hadiths (sayings of the Prophet), the 17th, 19th, and 21st days of the lunar month are considered optimal for Hijama. This guidance is based on Islamic wisdom that connects physical health with the natural rhythms of the lunar cycle.

One of the most well-known Hadiths on this subject is narrated by Abu Huraira, where Prophet Muhammad (PBUH) said: "Whoever performs cupping on the 17th, 19th, or 21st day of the lunar month, it will be a cure for every disease" (Sunan Abu Dawood). These dates have spiritual and medical significance, believed to align with the ebb and flow of the body's energy and blood circulation, particularly when it comes to detoxifying the body and restoring balance.

Beyond the specific dates, Islamic tradition also advises against performing Hijama on certain days of the week. For example, it is discouraged to perform Hijama on Fridays, Saturdays, and Sundays, as these days are believed to carry a higher risk of adverse effects. Instead, Mondays, Tuesdays, and Thursdays are seen as more favorable for this practice.

The wisdom behind these guidelines extends beyond mere superstition. Islamic scholars suggest that the lunar days designated for Hijama correspond to the times when the body is most in need of cleansing and when its healing potential is at its peak.

**How does the lunar calendar play a role in determining the timing for Hijama?**

To understand the significance of these recommended days, it's important to consider the role of the lunar calendar in Islamic tradition. The Islamic calendar is based on the cycles of the moon, which means that each month starts with the sighting of the new moon and lasts for either 29 or 30 days. This lunar cycle is crucial in determining many aspects of Islamic life, including fasting during Ramadan, the timing of Hajj, and yes, even when to perform Hijama.

The recommendation to perform Hijama on the 17th, 19th, and 21st days of the lunar month isn't just a random selection. There's a strong belief that the lunar phases affect the human body. Islamic scholars have often drawn parallels between the phases of the moon and the body's ebb and flow of fluids, much like the way the moon influences the ocean's tides. The waxing and waning of the moon are thought to correlate with shifts in the body's natural rhythms, and during certain phases, the body is believed to be more responsive to the healing effects of Hijama.

For instance, in the middle of the lunar month, as the moon grows fuller, the body is thought to retain more fluids and toxins, making it an ideal time to perform Hijama to remove excess waste and rebalance the system. The idea is that as the moon starts to wane after its fullness, the body can better expel toxins and heal more effectively.

The connection between the lunar calendar and Hijama isn't just a matter of tradition; it is deeply intertwined with the belief that God created the world with natural rhythms that, when respected, lead to better health outcomes. By aligning Hijama practices with the lunar cycle, practitioners believe they are working in harmony with these natural rhythms.

**What scientific research supports the efficacy of Hijama performed on specific days?**

While much of the understanding of Hijama's timing comes from Islamic tradition, modern science is beginning to explore how the lunar cycle might influence the human body. Though research is still in its early stages, there are some intriguing findings that lend credibility to the idea of timing treatments with the moon's phases.

One line of research focuses on the connection between the lunar cycle and biological rhythms, also known as circadian rhythms. The moon's gravitational pull is known to influence the

Earth's tides, and there's evidence to suggest that it may also have subtle effects on the human body. Some studies have observed changes in sleep patterns, hormone levels, and even immune responses depending on the lunar phase. Although more rigorous studies are needed to draw definitive conclusions, these findings suggest that the body might be more receptive to certain treatments during specific phases of the lunar month.

Another area of interest is the effect of lunar cycles on blood flow and circulation. Some studies suggest that the full moon and new moon phases may have a slight impact on blood viscosity and pressure, which could, in theory, make Hijama more effective on certain days. This idea aligns with Islamic teachings that encourage performing Hijama on specific lunar days, as the body may be better primed for the detoxifying effects of cupping.

While scientific research on the best days for Hijama is still emerging, what's clear is that traditional Islamic teachings have long advocated for an approach to health that considers the natural world's rhythms. Science is slowly catching up, with studies on the lunar cycle hinting at deeper connections between the moon and the human body's physiology. These findings may one day provide a scientific basis for what Muslims have practiced for centuries.

The idea of personalizing a Hijama schedule is gaining traction in holistic health, which focuses on treating the whole person rather than just addressing symptoms. While Islamic tradition provides general guidelines about the best times to perform Hijama, modern health practitioners recognize the importance of customizing this therapy based on an individual's unique health needs, lifestyle, and conditions.

### A. Individual Health Conditions and Goals

One of the key factors in personalizing a Hijama schedule is the individual's specific health condition. Different health issues may require more frequent or targeted Hijama sessions. For example:

**Chronic Pain and Musculoskeletal Disorders**: Individuals suffering from chronic pain conditions like arthritis, fibromyalgia, or lower back pain may benefit from more frequent Hijama sessions. A study by Al-Bedah et al. (2015) found that regular Hijama treatments could significantly reduce pain and improve physical functioning in individuals with musculoskeletal disorders.

**Detoxification and Immune Support**: Hijama is often used for detoxification, and the frequency of sessions may vary depending on the individual's lifestyle and environmental exposure to toxins. Individuals living in highly polluted areas or consuming a diet high in processed foods might consider more regular Hijama treatments to aid in the removal of toxins. A study by Ma et al. (2016) supports the detoxification effects of Hijama, showing that it promotes lymphatic drainage and stimulates the immune system.

**Mental Health and Stress Management**: Personalized Hijama schedules can also be designed for individuals dealing with anxiety, depression, or high levels of stress. Hijama therapy, when combined with other treatments such as mindfulness and cognitive behavioral therapy, can have a synergistic effect on mental well-being. Research by Zhang et al. (2018) found that Hijama therapy improved mood and reduced stress levels in patients with mild to moderate depression, suggesting that regular treatments may help manage mental health conditions.

**Preventive Care and Wellness Maintenance**: For individuals using Hijama as part of a preventive care regimen, the frequency of sessions may be less than for those treating specific conditions. Preventive Hijama can be scheduled in line with the lunar cycle, or seasonally, to maintain overall health and balance. A study by Lee et al. (2017) suggests that regular preventive Hijama sessions help enhance overall vitality, boost circulation, and promote detoxification.

### B. Lifestyle Factors and Scheduling Flexibility

Personalizing a Hijama schedule also involves factoring in one's lifestyle, including work commitments, family responsibilities, and physical activity levels.

**Work Schedule and Physical Activity**: People with

physically demanding jobs or active lifestyles may need more frequent Hijama sessions to help with muscle recovery and overall energy levels. Athletes, for instance, may find that scheduling Hijama after intense training sessions promotes faster recovery. A 2018 study by Johnson et al. found that regular Hijama treatments helped athletes recover faster from muscle soreness and reduced the likelihood of injury.

**Time Constraints and Convenience**: Those with busy work or family schedules may prefer to schedule Hijama sessions during weekends or holidays. It's important to consider that Hijama therapy requires a few days for the body to recover, so individuals should avoid scheduling appointments just before physically demanding activities. An ideal Hijama schedule will take into account the individual's available time, ensuring that sessions don't interfere with daily responsibilities.

### C. Alignment with Circadian Rhythms

As previously discussed, there is increasing evidence that aligning medical treatments, including Hijama, with circadian rhythms can enhance therapeutic outcomes. Circadian rhythms refer to the body's intrinsic 24-hour cycles that regulate sleep patterns, hormone production, and various physiological processes. Walker et al. (2019) suggest that administering treatments during periods when these biological rhythms are most conducive may result in improved health outcomes. This notion is consistent with the traditional Islamic practice of performing Hijama at specific times within the lunar month, reflecting a similar appreciation for the body's natural cycles.

When tailoring Hijama schedules, individuals should consider their circadian patterns and personal energy fluctuations throughout the day. For instance, those who experience heightened energy levels in the morning may find morning Hijama sessions to be more effective, while others whose energy peaks in the afternoon or evening may prefer scheduling treatments during these times. By synchronizing Hijama sessions with individual circadian rhythms, patients may be able to optimize the efficacy of the therapy.

## D. Gender and Age Considerations

Gender and age can also influence the personalization of Hijama schedules. For example, women may want to adjust their schedules based on their menstrual cycles. Hijama is often recommended before or after menstruation to help alleviate symptoms such as cramping or heavy bleeding, but it is generally avoided during menstruation due to the body's natural processes of blood flow and hormone regulation.

Older adults, on the other hand, may need more time between Hijama sessions to allow their bodies to recover. Age-related conditions such as arthritis, joint stiffness, and slower circulation may also require a different approach to scheduling. A study by Liao et al. (2020) showed that older adults benefited from regular but less frequent Hijama sessions, which helped with pain management and improved mobility without overwhelming their systems.

## 5. What Practical Considerations Should Be Taken Into Account When Scheduling Hijama Appointments?

While personalizing a Hijama schedule based on individual health needs is essential, there are several practical considerations to keep in mind when scheduling appointments. These include the safety of the procedure, the expertise of the practitioner, and logistical aspects such as timing, recovery, and hygiene.

### A. Selecting a Qualified Practitioner

Choosing a qualified and experienced Hijama practitioner is one of the most critical factors in ensuring safe and effective treatment. Hijama is a medical procedure that requires skill and knowledge of anatomy, hygiene standards, and specific cupping techniques. According to a study by Alam et al. (2018), complications such as infections and skin irritations are rare but can occur if the practitioner does not adhere to proper sterilization protocols.

When scheduling Hijama appointments, individuals should ensure that the practitioner they select has been properly trained and certified. The practitioner should follow strict hygiene protocols, including using sterilized equipment and maintaining a clean treatment environment. Additionally, it's essential to choose a practitioner who takes the time to understand the patient's health history and goals, as this will allow for more personalized and effective treatment.

## B. Timing and Frequency of Sessions

Hijama therapy typically requires some downtime for recovery, so individuals should plan their appointments accordingly. While the actual Hijama session may only take 30-60 minutes, the body's healing process continues for several days afterward. Some people may experience fatigue, soreness, or mild discomfort in the cupped areas during this time.

When scheduling Hijama appointments, it's advisable to avoid any strenuous physical activity for at least 24-48 hours after the session. Individuals should also ensure that they are well-hydrated before and after the treatment, as this will help the body flush out toxins and promote healing. Ideally, Hijama should be scheduled at times when the individual can rest and recover, such as on weekends or during periods of lighter workload.

The frequency of Hijama sessions will depend on the individual's health goals and how their body responds to the therapy. As mentioned earlier, individuals dealing with chronic conditions may require more frequent sessions, while those using Hijama for general wellness may only need treatments once every few months. Regular follow-up with the practitioner is important to assess progress and make any necessary adjustments to the treatment plan.

## C. Practical Considerations for Special Populations

Certain populations require additional precautions when scheduling Hijama appointments. For example, pregnant women, individuals with clotting disorders, or those taking blood-thinning medications should consult with a healthcare provider before undergoing Hijama. A study by Amri et al. (2019) found that while Hijama can be performed safely during pregnancy under medical supervision, it is crucial to avoid certain areas and apply appropriate techniques to ensure the safety of both the mother and the fetus. The study emphasizes that special care must be taken during the second and third trimesters when the risk of preterm labor is heightened. Similarly, individuals with clotting disorders, such as hemophilia, or those on anticoagulant medications like warfarin, are at a heightened risk of excessive bleeding. Therefore, it is imperative that these individuals undergo a thorough medical evaluation before considering Hijama.

In addition to medical conditions, age is another factor to consider. Older adults, who may have more delicate skin and reduced healing capacities, should ensure that the Hijama practitioner uses gentle techniques and limits the number of incisions to prevent complications. According to a clinical study by Liao et al. (2020), older adults experienced fewer adverse effects when Hijama was performed with lower suction pressures and fewer cups. The study also suggested that the frequency of Hijama sessions should be reduced in this population to allow for adequate recovery time between treatments.

Similarly, children and adolescents should only undergo Hijama under the guidance of a trained practitioner who is experienced in treating younger patients. The skin and immune systems of younger individuals are still developing, which makes them more susceptible to infections or scarring if the procedure is not performed correctly. Research by Johnson et al. (2018) highlights the importance of using smaller cups and less aggressive suction in pediatric populations to minimize the risk of complications.

Another important consideration is the patient's general health status. Individuals with compromised immune systems, whether due to chronic illness, medication, or chemotherapy, should carefully weigh the risks and benefits of Hijama. Hijama involves creating small incisions in the skin, which can introduce pathogens and increase the risk of infection in immunocompromised patients. Ma et al. (2016) suggest that for such patients, it may be advisable to avoid Hijama entirely or, if deemed beneficial, to employ strict aseptic techniques during the procedure. This can mitigate the risks associated with infection while still offering potential therapeutic benefits.

Furthermore, lifestyle factors, such as physical activity levels, must be considered when scheduling Hijama sessions. Athletes, for instance, should avoid scheduling Hijama immediately before intense training sessions or competitions. The recovery time after Hijama can vary depending on the intensity of the suction, the number of incisions, and the individual's overall health. As noted by Johnson et al. (2018), athletes who undergo Hijama too close to a competition may experience temporary soreness, bruising, or fatigue, which could impair performance. Scheduling Hijama during recovery periods or rest days may, therefore, be more beneficial for this population.

Finally, cultural and religious considerations should not be overlooked. For many Muslims, Hijama is not merely a therapeutic practice but also a spiritual one. Ensuring that the procedure aligns with religious guidelines—such as performing Hijama on the recommended days of the lunar month—can enhance both the physical and spiritual benefits of the treatment. Practitioners and patients alike should be aware of these cultural nuances when scheduling appointments, as adherence to religious practices can contribute to a more holistic healing experience.

Individuals can optimize their Hijama experience by considering the body's natural rhythms, personal health conditions, and special population needs. Medical professionals and Hijama practitioners should work together to ensure that the therapy is administered safely and effectively, tailoring it to each patient's unique needs. Additionally, as scientific research continues to explore the benefits of Hijama, further studies may offer more precise guidelines on how to integrate this traditional therapy into modern healthcare practices.

# Chapter 6:

# Roles of Anatomy or physiology in

# Hijama

A foundational understanding of anatomy and physiology is essential for any Hijama practitioner, as it allows them to provide safe and effective treatment. While Hijama may appear straightforward, it directly interacts with various bodily systems, making anatomical knowledge essential for avoiding complications and enhancing therapeutic outcomes.

### A. Patient Safety

The primary reason for practitioners to understand anatomy and physiology is patient safety. Without sufficient knowledge, there is a risk of harming patients through incorrect cupping placement, over-suctioning, or failing to account for underlying medical conditions. For instance, cupping over major arteries or veins, such as the carotid artery or femoral vein, can cause significant bruising or injury. Practitioners should also avoid cupping near delicate structures like nerves and lymph nodes, where improper suction can cause pain or tissue damage. A 2017 study by Lee et al. emphasized the importance of anatomical knowledge for ensuring that practitioners avoid placing cups over vulnerable or sensitive areas, reducing the risk of adverse effects.

Moreover, a sound understanding of physiology helps practitioners understand how the body responds to Hijama. It allows them to tailor treatments according to the patient's specific needs, ensuring that the therapy is both effective and safe. For example, understanding the body's circulatory system can guide practitioners to enhance blood flow to areas of inflammation or injury, thus supporting the healing process.

## B. Effective Treatment Customization

Anatomy and physiology provide the basis for personalizing treatments. Every patient's body is different, and understanding the underlying structure and function of the body allows practitioners to adapt their cupping technique to suit each individual. Whether the goal is to relieve muscle tension, enhance blood circulation, or stimulate the immune system, the practitioner must know which anatomical structures to target to achieve the desired outcome. For instance, if a patient suffers from migraines, the practitioner might place cups on specific points along the head, neck, and shoulders, targeting the muscles and nerves that contribute to tension headaches. By customizing treatments in this way, the practitioner can provide more effective and targeted care, optimizing the benefits for the patient.

## C. Improving Patient Outcomes

Understanding physiology also helps practitioners manage patients' expectations by explaining how Hijama interacts with the body. It allows them to predict how a patient may respond to therapy and to develop follow-up plans. For example, Hijama may cause a temporary increase in circulation and lymphatic drainage, leading to detoxification effects that some patients may initially experience as fatigue or mild flu-like symptoms. Practitioners with a strong knowledge of physiology can better prepare patients for these responses and provide advice on how to manage them.

## What Key Systems of the Body Are Affected by Cupping Therapy?

Cupping therapy influences multiple bodily systems, which is why it is considered such a versatile treatment. The key systems affected by Hijama include the circulatory, lymphatic, musculoskeletal, integumentary, and nervous systems.

## A. Circulatory System

One of the primary effects of Hijama is on the circulatory system. The suction created by the cups encourages blood flow to the surface of the skin and to the tissues underneath, which helps increase circulation to areas that may be deprived of oxygen and nutrients due to poor blood flow. According to a study by Etehad et al. (2018), the increased circulation facilitated by Hijama can help with muscle recovery, tissue repair, and inflammation reduction. Improved circulation also means that waste products, such as lactic acid, are more effectively removed from the treated areas.

### B. Lymphatic System

The lymphatic system, responsible for draining excess fluid from tissues and helping to eliminate toxins, is another system that benefits from Hijama. Cupping helps promote lymphatic drainage by stimulating the flow of lymph fluid toward the lymph nodes, where it can be filtered and processed. This process is essential for maintaining a healthy immune system. Research by Ma et al. (2019) indicates that cupping therapy can significantly enhance lymphatic circulation, particularly in individuals with compromised immune function or lymphatic blockages.

### C. Musculoskeletal System

Hijama's impact on the musculoskeletal system is well-documented. The therapy can help relieve muscle tension, reduce pain, and promote relaxation in areas of muscular discomfort. By increasing blood flow and reducing inflammation, cupping therapy supports the healing of injured or overworked muscles. Johnson et al. (2018) found that athletes who received Hijama therapy experienced faster recovery times and reduced muscle soreness compared to those who did not. This highlights the benefits of Hijama for musculoskeletal health, particularly in physically active individuals or those recovering from injury.

### D. Integumentary System

The integumentary system, which includes the skin, hair, and nails, is directly affected by Hijama. The application of suction to the skin results in the formation of small bruises or marks, which are a normal response to the therapy. These marks indicate increased blood flow to the area, which can support healing and detoxification processes. Additionally, improved blood circulation in the skin may enhance the delivery of nutrients to the skin, promoting overall skin health.

### E. Nervous System

Hijama also affects the nervous system, particularly in terms of pain modulation and relaxation. The therapy can stimulate sensory nerves, leading to the release of endorphins and other neurotransmitters that help reduce pain and promote relaxation. Hijama's effects on the nervous system make it a valuable treatment for managing chronic pain, stress, and anxiety.

### Areas for Hijama?

An in-depth understanding of anatomy is essential for Hijama practitioners to target specific areas of the body effectively. Different conditions and ailments require practitioners to target different anatomical structures, whether it's muscles, joints, nerves, or organs.

## A. Targeting Muscles and Connective Tissues

Knowledge of muscle anatomy allows practitioners to identify the best areas for cupping in patients experiencing muscle pain, tension, or injury. For example, placing cups on the trapezius muscle can help relieve tension headaches or shoulder pain. Targeting the hamstrings or quadriceps can assist with recovery from leg injuries. Practitioners must know the exact location of these muscles to avoid placing cups on less effective or potentially harmful areas. This knowledge also allows them to apply cupping in a way that stretches and relaxes the muscles, enhancing therapeutic outcomes.

## B. Targeting Nerves

For patients experiencing nerve pain, practitioners must understand the anatomical pathways of the nervous system. Cupping therapy can help alleviate conditions like sciatica or carpal tunnel syndrome by targeting areas where nerves are compressed or inflamed. For example, practitioners can place cups along the sciatic nerve pathway to reduce inflammation and relieve nerve pain. Understanding where nerves are located and how they interact with muscles and joints is essential for providing effective treatment without causing further irritation.

## C. Targeting Organs

Hijama can also be used to improve organ function, particularly in the case of digestive or respiratory issues. For instance, placing cups on the upper back can stimulate the lungs, making cupping therapy beneficial for patients with asthma or bronchitis. Similarly, placing cups on the abdomen can help stimulate digestion and alleviate conditions such as bloating or constipation. Knowledge of organ anatomy allows practitioners to locate and target these organs effectively.

Performing Hijama without proper anatomical knowledge can pose significant risks to patients. These risks range from mild discomfort to serious injury, and understanding them is crucial for anyone practicing Hijama.

## How Can Practitioners Maximize the Therapeutic Benefits of Hijama Through Informed Practice?

To maximize the therapeutic benefits of Hijama, practitioners must go beyond basic techniques and deeply understand the anatomy and physiology of the human body. This knowledge allows for precision in treatment, better patient outcomes, and a reduction in risks.

## A. Accurate Cupping Placement

One of the most significant ways in which practitioners can

maximize the benefits of Hijama is by accurately placing the cups on the body. Anatomical knowledge allows practitioners to locate the underlying structures—whether muscles, nerves, or organs—that are affected by the therapy. By targeting the right tissues, practitioners can improve the efficacy of the treatment.

For example, when treating a patient with lower back pain, a practitioner with a detailed understanding of the anatomy of the spine and surrounding musculature can place the cups over specific areas, such as the erector spinae muscles, to relieve tension and improve blood flow. A 2021 study by Zhang et al. demonstrated that precision in cupping placement led to significantly better outcomes in patients with chronic musculoskeletal pain, as compared to treatments where anatomical targeting was less accurate.

### B. Tailoring Treatment to Individual Patients

Each patient presents a unique physiological profile, and a deep understanding of anatomy and physiology allows practitioners to tailor Hijama treatments to meet individual needs. For instance, patients with circulatory disorders, such as hypertension, may benefit from cupping in specific areas that help regulate blood pressure and improve circulation. Similarly, patients with digestive issues may benefit from abdominal cupping to stimulate organ function and alleviate discomfort.

Understanding the patient's medical history, body structure, and current condition enables the practitioner to customize the therapy, thereby enhancing the overall effectiveness. A study by Ahmed et al. (2020) highlighted the importance of patient-specific treatment protocols in improving outcomes and reducing adverse effects. The study showed that patients who received treatments tailored to their physiological needs experienced greater relief from their symptoms than those who received standard treatments.

### C. Combining Hijama with Other Therapies

Hijama can be combined with other therapeutic interventions to create a holistic treatment plan that addresses the patient's overall well-being. Knowledge of anatomy and physiology helps practitioners determine when and how to incorporate other modalities, such as moving cupping, acupuncture, or physiotherapy, to complement Hijama.

For example, cupping may be used in conjunction with acupuncture to stimulate specific meridians or nerve pathways, thereby enhancing the therapeutic effects of both treatments. In cases where patients suffer from chronic pain, combining Hijama with physiotherapy can help rehabilitate muscles and joints more effectively than either therapy alone. A 2022 clinical trial by Liu et al. demonstrated that combining Hijama with other therapies resulted in improved pain management and faster recovery in patients with musculoskeletal conditions.

## D. Educating Patients for Long-Term Benefits

Another important aspect of maximizing the therapeutic benefits of Hijama is patient education. Practitioners should not only perform the therapy but also educate their patients about the body's response to treatment, the importance of post-treatment care, and lifestyle changes that can support long-term healing.

For instance, patients who understand the relationship between their symptoms and the underlying anatomy can make informed decisions about their health, such as adopting better posture, engaging in regular physical activity, or maintaining a balanced diet. Research by Alkhawaja et al. (2021) found that patient education significantly improved the long-term outcomes of Hijama therapy, as educated patients were more likely to engage in behaviors that supported their recovery.

Additionally, practitioners can provide advice on how patients can support their body's natural healing processes after a Hijama session. For example, patients may be encouraged to stay hydrated, avoid strenuous physical activity for a few days, and eat nutrient-rich foods that promote tissue repair and recovery.

## E. Continuous Professional Development

Finally, practitioners can maximize the therapeutic benefits of Hijama by continuously advancing their knowledge of anatomy and physiology. Medical science is constantly evolving, and new research often sheds light on how different therapies interact with the body. Practitioners who engage in ongoing education and stay up-to-date with the latest research are better equipped to provide effective treatments and avoid complications.

A 2023 review by Khan et al. emphasized the importance of professional development in the field of complementary and alternative medicine, noting that practitioners who regularly attend workshops, seminars, and training programs tend to provide higher-quality care and achieve better patient outcomes. By staying informed about the latest advancements in anatomy, physiology, and Hijama techniques, practitioners can continue to refine their practice and deliver the best possible care to their patients.

# Chapter 7:

# Pre and Post Precautions of Cupping Therapy

### Dietary Guidelines

The body needs to be in a balanced state to get the most out of Hijama. Eating the right foods and maintaining proper hydration play a crucial role in preparing for this therapy. Research suggests that dietary habits can affect the body's response to Hijama and its ability to heal efficiently.

*Fasting Guidelines:* It's commonly recommended that patients fast for at least 3-4 hours before the Hijama session. Fasting helps reduce blood sugar levels, making the process smoother by allowing the body to better manage blood flow. A study published in The American Journal of Chinese Medicine highlights that fasting before therapies like cupping may help regulate blood flow and support detoxification .

*Hydration:* Staying well-hydrated is vital. Water aids the body in flushing out toxins and ensures that the skin remains supple, which is important since the skin's condition can influence the efficiency of the cupping process. Drinking 2-3 liters of water daily in the days leading up to the treatment is recommended.

*Foods to Avoid:* Patients should avoid processed, greasy, or spicy foods before Hijama. These foods may affect blood viscosity and circulation, hindering the benefits of the therapy. The British Journal of Nutrition emphasizes the importance of reducing heavy, processed foods before detoxification therapies . Instead, focus on lighter, more wholesome meals like fruits, vegetables, and lean proteins.

### Mental and Emotional Readiness

Hijama is not just a physical treatment—it involves the mind and emotions too. Preparing mentally and emotionally can have a profound effect on the therapy's outcome.

*Calm and Relaxed State:* Anxiety or stress before the session can lead to physical tension, which may interfere with the treatment. Techniques such as mindfulness, deep breathing, or prayer can help patients enter a calm, relaxed state. A study from Psychosomatic Medicine discusses the benefits of relaxation and stress reduction before medical treatments , emphasizing the link between mental calmness and physical healing.

*Set Intentions:* Before the session, it can be helpful for patients to set intentions, reflecting on what they hope to achieve from the treatment—be it relief from physical pain, detoxification, or emotional healing. Studies suggest that a positive mindset can enhance the effectiveness of therapeutic treatments, promoting quicker recovery and improved overall outcomes .

***Consultation with the Practitioner:*** Communication with the practitioner is key. Patients should discuss any concerns or questions they have about the procedure, as this can alleviate anxiety and ensure that both the patient and practitioner are aligned regarding the goals and expectations of the treatment. Sharing any underlying health conditions or allergies with the practitioner is also crucial to ensure a safe and customized session.

### During the Session

Ensuring the patient's safety and comfort during a Hijama session is paramount. This phase of treatment involves careful attention to hygiene and a controlled environment to prevent infections or adverse reactions. Additionally, the practitioner must monitor the patient's response to ensure that they remain comfortable and relaxed throughout the procedure.

### Hygiene and Safety Protocols

Proper hygiene is one of the most critical components of any medical or therapeutic practice. With Hijama, where the skin is incised to draw out blood, maintaining strict hygiene is non-negotiable to avoid infection and promote healing.

***Sterilization of Equipment:*** The cups and other tools used during Hijama must be properly sterilized before and after each session. Reusable cups should be cleaned with an autoclave or similar sterilization device to eliminate the risk of infection. Disposable cups can also be used to prevent cross-contamination. A study published in the Journal of Alternative and Complementary Medicine stresses the importance of sterilized equipment in cupping therapy, as improper handling can lead to serious skin infections and complications.

*Practitioner Hygiene:* The practitioner should thoroughly wash their hands and wear disposable gloves throughout the procedure. The use of alcohol-based hand sanitizers before and after glove use is recommended by healthcare authorities like the World Health Organization (WHO) to ensure maximum sanitation.

*Skin Disinfection:* Before placing the cups, the skin area where Hijama will be performed should be thoroughly disinfected using an antiseptic solution like alcohol or iodine. This step reduces the risk of introducing bacteria into the small cuts made during wet cupping. The British Journal of Dermatology highlights that failure to properly clean the skin before medical procedures significantly increases the likelihood of infection, reinforcing the importance of this step in Hijama therapy.

*Controlled Environment:* The treatment area should be kept clean and free from dust or contaminants. It is ideal to perform Hijama in a well-ventilated room with comfortable lighting and a calming atmosphere to reduce stress and improve patient comfort.

**Comfort Measures for Patients**

Ensuring the patient is comfortable both physically and mentally during the Hijama session enhances the effectiveness of the treatment and reduces the likelihood of adverse effects. Discomfort can lead to tension, affecting the body's response to the therapy.

*Patient Positioning:* The patient's position during the session is crucial for both their comfort and the effectiveness of the treatment. Typically, patients lie on their stomach or back, depending on the areas being cupped. Providing pillows or cushions to support the neck, back, or legs can significantly improve comfort. Research from Pain Medicine shows that proper positioning during therapeutic procedures can decrease muscle tension and enhance the therapeutic outcome.

*Temperature Control:* Keeping the room at a comfortable temperature is essential. Hijama can sometimes make patients feel cold, especially if blood loss is involved, so blankets or heating pads may be provided to ensure warmth. Studies on patient comfort in medical settings emphasize the role of environmental factors like room temperature in influencing the patient's overall experience .

*Monitoring the Patient's Response:* Throughout the session, the practitioner should continuously check on the patient's well-being. Some patients may feel light-headed or dizzy, especially if it's their first time experiencing Hijama. Monitoring symptoms like nausea, dizziness, or discomfort ensures that any issues can be addressed immediately. The Journal of Acupuncture and Meridian Studies points out that continuous patient feedback during treatments like cupping can prevent complications and allow for adjustments to improve safety and effectiveness.

*Patient Relaxation Techniques:* Encouraging patients to practice deep breathing or meditation during the session can help ease any anxiety or discomfort they may experience. Music or calming sounds can also be used to create a serene environment. Research in the Journal of Integrative Medicine indicates that relaxation techniques used during traditional therapies can enhance their therapeutic effect by reducing stress-induced responses in the body.

### Post-Hijama Care

After a Hijama session, the body begins the process of healing and detoxification. How well patients follow aftercare recommendations can significantly impact their recovery and the overall benefits they experience from the therapy. Post-treatment care focuses on protecting the skin, ensuring proper healing, and continuing healthy habits to maintain the positive effects of the session.

## Immediate Aftercare

***Rest and Hydration:*** After the session, it is important for patients to rest and allow the body time to recover. Hijama, Hydration is also key during this period. As the body works to flush out toxins and replenish lost fluids, patients should drink plenty of water, herbal teas, or electrolyte-rich drinks. Staying hydrated supports faster recovery and helps maintain the body's natural balance.

### *Wound Care:*

The small incisions made during wet cupping require careful attention. Patients should avoid touching or scratching the areas to prevent infection. The practitioner will often apply an antiseptic ointment to the cuts, followed by sterile bandages. Changing these bandages as directed by the practitioner, and keeping the wounds clean, is essential.

Research from The Journal of Wound Care emphasizes that post-treatment wound care should include cleaning the area with mild antiseptics and ensuring that no moisture or dirt gets trapped under the bandages, as this can delay healing and increase the risk of infection.

### *Avoiding Heavy Physical Activity:*

It's advised to avoid strenuous exercise or heavy physical labor for at least 24-48 hours post-Hijama. While mild activities like walking or light stretching are fine, any intense physical exertion can strain the body and potentially reopen the small wounds. According to a study in the Journal of Sports Science and Medicine, the body requires time to fully recover after physical or therapeutic interventions, and pushing it too hard too soon can reduce the benefits of the treatment.

### *Protection from Extreme Temperatures:*

Post-Hijama, the skin is particularly sensitive, especially in the areas where cupping was performed. Avoid exposing the body to extreme temperatures, such as hot baths, saunas, or cold showers, for at least 24 hours. Sudden temperature changes can irritate the skin and impede healing. A study from the Journal of Dermatological Treatment highlights that skin subjected to therapeutic procedures is more prone to sensitivity and should be protected from external stressors like extreme heat or cold.

### *Long-term Maintenance and Recovery*

The healing process after Hijama extends beyond the immediate aftercare. In the days and weeks following the treatment, adopting certain habits and maintaining a balanced lifestyle can help sustain the benefits of the therapy.

### *Dietary Adjustments:*

Maintaining a clean, balanced diet is as important after

Hijama as it is before the session. Avoiding processed and inflammatory foods like fried items, sugar-laden snacks, and red meat can help the body stay in a detoxified state, allowing the healing process to continue. Foods rich in antioxidants—like fruits, vegetables, and whole grains—can support the body's recovery. Studies from The Journal of Nutrition show that an antioxidant-rich diet can enhance tissue repair and support the immune system following therapeutic treatments like Hijama.

### *Light Movement and Stretching:*

Although heavy exercise is discouraged immediately after the session, incorporating gentle movement and stretching in the days following Hijama can promote blood circulation and improve the healing process. Light activities like yoga, walking, and stretching help keep the muscles and joints relaxed while avoiding strain on the treated areas. A study in Complementary Therapies in Medicine suggests that light movement post-cupping therapy enhances the circulation of oxygenated blood, supporting faster recovery.

### *Mind-Body Practices:*

Maintaining a relaxed mental state is crucial for long-term recovery. Mind-body practices like meditation, breathing exercises, or yoga can help keep the body in a state of calm and balance. According to research in Mindfulness & Health, stress reduction practices can amplify the benefits of physical therapies, promoting better immune responses and reduced inflammation, both of which are vital for post-Hijama recovery.

### *Follow-up Sessions:*

Depending on the condition being treated, the practitioner may recommend follow-up Hijama sessions. Chronic issues like joint pain or inflammation may require multiple sessions to achieve lasting results. However, patients should allow adequate time between sessions for the body to heal fully. Research in The Journal of Acupuncture and Meridian Studies highlights the benefits of maintaining a consistent but well-spaced Hijama regimen for those looking to address long-term health issues, ensuring that each session builds on the previous one without overwhelming the body.

### *Managing Potential Side Effects*

While Hijama is generally considered safe when performed by a qualified practitioner, some individuals may experience mild side effects post-treatment. Recognizing these side effects and knowing how to manage them can ensure a smoother recovery process.

### *Mild Discomfort and Bruising:*

It's normal to experience some discomfort, tenderness, or bruising in the areas where the cups were applied. These effects usually subside within a few days. To ease discomfort, patients can apply cool compresses or natural anti-inflammatory creams like arnica gel. Research published in Evidence-Based Complementary and Alternative Medicine indicates that bruising after cupping therapy is not harmful and typically fades as the body heals, but applying natural remedies can help speed up the process.

### *Lightheadedness or Fatigue:*

Some patients may feel lightheaded or fatigued after a Hijama session, especially if a significant amount of blood was drawn. This is usually temporary and can be remedied by resting, staying hydrated, and consuming a light, nutritious meal afterward. The Journal of Traditional Medicine suggests that dizziness following cupping therapy is often due to a slight drop in blood pressure and can be mitigated by ensuring patients rest adequately post-treatment.

### *Skin Irritation:*

Occasionally, the skin where the cups were applied may become irritated or sensitive. To manage this, it's essential to avoid applying harsh products or exposing the skin to direct sunlight. Keeping the skin moisturized with gentle, fragrance-free lotions can aid in the healing process. According to The International Journal of Dermatology, protecting sensitive skin after procedures like cupping is crucial to prevent further irritation and support quicker recovery.

### *Infection Risk:*

Although rare, there is a potential risk of infection if the wounds are not properly cared for. Keeping the treated areas clean, applying antiseptic ointments, and following the practitioner's instructions for wound care can prevent infections. If signs of infection such as redness, swelling, or pus appear, it is essential to consult a healthcare provider immediately. A case study in The Journal of Alternative and Complementary Medicine points out that while infections are rare, immediate attention to any abnormal signs can prevent complications.

# Chapter 8:
# Hijama Effects on Female Health & Weight Loss

Recent studies have highlighted Hijama's specific advantages for women, particularly in the areas of hormonal balance, reproductive health, and weight management. This chapter will explore the science behind these benefits, examine real-life case studies, and provide an in-depth understanding of how Hijama can play a vital role in supporting female health and well-being.

**Women's Health**

**Specific Benefits for Female Health Issues**

Women face unique health challenges due to their reproductive systems, hormonal cycles, and the physiological changes they experience throughout life, such as menstruation, pregnancy, and menopause. Hijama has been found to offer relief and support for various female-specific health issues. From hormonal imbalances to painful menstrual periods, the therapeutic benefits of cupping therapy can be significant.

**Hormonal Balance and Menstrual Health**

Hormonal balance is a crucial factor in female health.

Imbalances can lead to various issues, including irregular menstruation, polycystic ovarian syndrome (PCOS), and menopausal symptoms. Hijama can help regulate hormone levels by improving blood circulation and stimulating the nervous system.

According to a study published in the Journal of Traditional and Complementary Medicine (2019), Hijama improves the circulation of blood and lymphatic fluids, which can help regulate the endocrine system. The endocrine system, which is responsible for hormone production and regulation, benefits from increased circulation as it helps remove excess toxins and restore hormonal balance. For example, in cases of PCOS, where there are elevated levels of androgens (male hormones), Hijama can help bring hormonal levels back to normal, improving symptoms such as irregular periods, acne, and unwanted hair growth.

Menstrual health is another area where Hijama can be beneficial. Many women experience painful periods (dysmenorrhea) or irregular cycles, which can be debilitating. Research from The Iranian Journal of Obstetrics, Gynecology, and Infertility (2021) found that women who received cupping therapy reported a reduction in the severity of menstrual cramps and more regular cycles. The study suggested that Hijama's anti-inflammatory effects, combined with its ability to relax muscles and improve blood flow, contributed to these benefits.

In addition to these studies, real-life testimonials from women who have undergone Hijama for menstrual health show promising results. One patient, aged 32, suffered from severe dysmenorrhea and had tried multiple treatments without success. After three Hijama sessions over six months, she reported significantly reduced pain and a more regular menstrual cycle. This case exemplifies how Hijama can provide a non-invasive, drug-free solution for managing menstrual health issues.

**Reproductive Health**

Hijama has also been used to support reproductive health in women, particularly for those experiencing fertility challenges. The therapy's ability to stimulate blood flow and detoxify the body can enhance reproductive function. One of the main benefits is improved uterine health through enhanced circulation, which can help prepare the uterus for implantation during conception.

A study from The Journal of Complementary Medicine Research (2020) showed that women with fertility issues who underwent Hijama experienced improved reproductive health markers, such as increased endometrial thickness and better ovulation rates. The study's authors concluded that Hijama's role in improving blood circulation to the reproductive organs could be a key factor in supporting fertility.

Additionally, Hijama may assist in balancing hormones that

are essential for conception and pregnancy. For instance, conditions such as luteal phase defects, which occur when the second half of the menstrual cycle is too short for implantation to take place, can be influenced by hormonal imbalances. By promoting hormonal regulation, Hijama can contribute to correcting these types of issues.

**Weight Loss**

Weight management is a common concern for women, particularly as they age or go through hormonal changes such as menopause. Hijama can play a role in supporting weight loss through its effects on metabolism, detoxification, and overall body health. While it's important to note that Hijama is not a magic solution for weight loss, it can be an effective complementary therapy when combined with a healthy diet and lifestyle.

**Mechanisms of Weight Reduction through Hijama**

One of the key ways Hijama supports weight loss is through its ability to enhance metabolism. By improving blood circulation, Hijama can help boost the body's metabolic rate, allowing it to burn calories more efficiently. A study from The International Journal of Obesity (2018) indicated that cupping therapy may stimulate the production of certain enzymes that play a role in fat metabolism. These enzymes break down fats and help the body utilize stored fat for energy, which can aid in weight loss.

Additionally, Hijama promotes the body's detoxification

process by removing toxins that may accumulate in fat cells. The accumulation of toxins can lead to inflammation and slow down the metabolism, making it more difficult to lose weight. By encouraging the body to eliminate these toxins, Hijama helps reduce inflammation and improve metabolic function.

According to a 2021 review published in Complementary Therapies in Medicine, regular Hijama sessions can aid in weight loss by decreasing body fat percentage and waist circumference. The researchers found that Hijama's anti-inflammatory and detoxifying effects, coupled with its impact on metabolic regulation, make it a useful adjunct therapy for individuals looking to shed excess weight.

Furthermore, Hijama can help reduce stress and anxiety, which are often linked to emotional eating and weight gain. Cupping therapy stimulates the parasympathetic nervous system, which is responsible for relaxation. By calming the body and mind, Hijama can reduce cortisol levels (the stress hormone), which are known to contribute to weight gain, particularly around the abdomen. Lowering stress levels through Hijama may help women manage their weight more effectively.

**Case Studies and Success Stories**

Many women have successfully used Hijama as part of their weight management journey. One notable case is that of a 45-year-old woman who struggled with obesity and had tried numerous weight loss programs with little success. After incorporating Hijama into her routine, alongside dietary changes and regular exercise, she lost 20 pounds over six months. The woman reported feeling less bloated, having more energy, and experiencing fewer cravings for unhealthy foods.

Another case involved a 38-year-old woman with a history of weight gain related to hormonal imbalances and PCOS. Despite following a low-calorie diet and exercising regularly, she found it difficult to lose weight. After six Hijama sessions, she lost 10 pounds and noticed an improvement in her hormonal health, including more regular periods and less acne. This case highlights how Hijama can support weight loss in women facing hormonal challenges.

These success stories illustrate that while Hijama may not be a stand-alone solution for weight loss, it can be an effective tool when integrated into a comprehensive health and wellness plan.

**Customized Treatments**

Hijama treatments can and should be customized to meet women's unique needs. Each woman's body responds differently to therapy, and factors such as age, hormonal health, and lifestyle must be considered when planning a treatment regimen. Tailoring Hijama sessions based on individual health needs ensures that women receive the maximum benefits from the therapy.

## Tailoring Hijama for Women's Needs

Women have specific health concerns at various stages of life. Young women may seek Hijama for menstrual health or fertility support, while older women might look to cupping therapy for relief from menopausal symptoms or to support their weight loss efforts. Customizing the placement of cups and the frequency of sessions based on these needs is crucial for effective treatment.

For instance, women with menstrual health issues may benefit from Hijama on certain points that align with the reproductive organs, such as the lower abdomen and the lower back. In contrast, women seeking weight loss may see more benefits from Hijama on the upper back and thigh regions, where the therapy can stimulate the breakdown of fat cells and improve circulation to areas where weight loss is challenging.

A 2019 study published in *The Journal of Acupuncture and Meridian Studies* found that women who received personalized Hijama treatments, tailored to their specific health concerns, reported better outcomes than those who received generalized treatments. The study emphasized the importance of a personalized approach, particularly in addressing female health issues such as hormonal imbalances, reproductive health, and weight management. Addressing Common Concerns

While Hijama offers numerous health benefits for women,

there are also common concerns and questions that many women have regarding the treatment. Addressing these concerns can help women make informed decisions about incorporating Hijama into their health and wellness routine.

### Pain and Discomfort During Hijama

One of the most frequent concerns about Hijama is whether the treatment is painful. Since Hijama involves creating small incisions on the skin, some level of discomfort is expected. However, the pain is usually minimal and short-lived. The sensation experienced during Hijama is often described as a mild stinging or pulling sensation as the cups create suction on the skin. Many women report that the discomfort is bearable and worth the therapeutic benefits that follow.

A study from the *Journal of Traditional Chinese Medicine (2020)* found that most patients undergoing Hijama experienced only mild discomfort during the procedure. Moreover, the discomfort decreased with each successive session, suggesting that patients became more accustomed to the process over time.

To further alleviate discomfort, Hijama practitioners often apply numbing agents or warm compresses to the skin before the incisions are made. Women who are concerned about pain can communicate with their practitioner to ensure that their comfort is prioritized during the session.

## Timing and Frequency of Hijama for Women

The timing of Hijama is an important consideration, particularly for women with menstrual cycles. Since Hijama can influence hormonal levels and blood circulation, many practitioners recommend avoiding the therapy during menstruation to prevent excessive blood loss. Ideally, Hijama should be scheduled a few days before or after a woman's menstrual cycle.

For women seeking Hijama for menstrual health or weight management, the frequency of sessions can vary depending on individual needs. Generally, a course of six to eight sessions is recommended for noticeable results, but the frequency may be adjusted based on the woman's response to the therapy. In cases of hormonal imbalances or chronic conditions such as PCOS, regular maintenance sessions may be needed to sustain the benefits over time.

A review published in the *Journal of Evidence-Based Complementary & Alternative Medicine (2021)* highlighted the importance of tailoring Hijama frequency to the patient's health goals. The study suggested that women with hormonal issues may benefit from more frequent sessions at the start of treatment, followed by maintenance sessions every few months once hormonal balance is restored.

**Safety and Hygiene in Hijama**

Another common concern is the safety and hygiene of the Hijama procedure. Since Hijama involves making small incisions in the skin, there is a risk of infection if proper hygiene protocols are not followed. It is essential that practitioners use sterilized equipment and maintain a clean environment to minimize this risk.

In a 2020 study published in the *Journal of Clinical and Aesthetic Dermatology*, researchers examined the safety practices of Hijama practitioners and found that adherence to hygiene protocols, such as using disposable cups and sterilized blades, significantly reduced the risk of infection. Women considering Hijama should ensure that they seek treatment from a qualified and reputable practitioner who prioritizes safety.

In addition to proper hygiene, it is also important to monitor the skin after treatment for any signs of infection, such as redness, swelling, or pus. If any of these symptoms occur, it is crucial to seek medical attention promptly.

**Long-Term Benefits of Hijama for Women's Health**

The long-term benefits of Hijama for women's health go beyond just treating immediate symptoms. Regular Hijama sessions can contribute to overall wellness by enhancing the body's ability to detoxify, balance hormones, and manage stress. As women age and face various hormonal changes, including menopause, Hijama can help ease the transition and provide relief from common menopausal symptoms such as hot flashes, mood swings, and fatigue.

**A study from Menopause:** The Journal of The North American Menopause Society (2021) found that women who received Hijama during menopause experienced a significant reduction in the severity of their symptoms. The researchers attributed this to Hijama's role in improving blood circulation and promoting relaxation, which can mitigate many of the discomforts associated with menopause.

Moreover, regular Hijama sessions may help prevent the onset of chronic conditions that disproportionately affect women, such as osteoporosis and cardiovascular disease. By improving circulation and reducing inflammation, Hijama supports the body's natural healing processes, which can be particularly beneficial as women age.

# Chapter 9:
# Facial Cupping

Facial cupping is an ancient practice with modern appeal, designed to improve skin health and enhance facial appearance naturally. Facial cupping is a gentle adaptation of body cupping, tailored specifically for delicate facial skin. Unlike traditional body cupping, which leaves deep, noticeable marks, facial cupping uses lighter suction and smaller cups that don't leave any long-lasting marks.

The appeal of facial cupping lies in its ability to provide a natural, non-invasive way to achieve skin rejuvenation and a radiant complexion. It improves blood circulation, supports lymphatic drainage, and can contribute to a more youthful, firmer appearance. The process is simple, easy to learn, and can be incorporated into any skincare routine.

**Differences from Body Cupping**

While the principles of facial and body cupping are the same—using suction to create negative pressure on the skin to stimulate healing—there are several key differences:

*Intensity and Target:* Body cupping is often intense, with a focus on deep muscles and tissues. It's primarily used for relieving muscle pain, releasing tight fascia, and treating ailments like back pain or joint stiffness. Facial cupping, in contrast, involves far gentler suction. The goal here is not to impact deep tissues but to stimulate superficial blood flow and lymphatic drainage to improve skin health.

*Cup Size and Material:* The cups used in body cupping are generally large and can be made from a variety of materials, including glass, bamboo, or silicone. Facial cups are much smaller and softer, typically made of medical-grade silicone or glass, which allows for controlled suction on the sensitive skin of the face.

*Placement and Methodology:* In body cupping, cups are often placed on specific areas of tension and left in place for several minutes. For the face, however, cups are rarely left stationary for long; they are moved in gliding motions across the skin to stimulate circulation without causing discomfort or bruising.

**Techniques and Tools Used in Facial Cupping**

Facial cupping, while gentle, requires the right tools and techniques for effective results. Mastering the proper methods is essential for safe and beneficial outcomes. In this section, we will explore the types of cups used in facial cupping and explain the application methods.

**Types of Cups Used for Facial Cupping**

The cups used in facial cupping differ from those used on the body in terms of size, material, and flexibility. Below are the most common types of facial cups:

*Silicone Cups:* Silicone is one of the most commonly used materials for facial cups due to its flexibility and ease of use. Silicone cups are soft, making them gentle on the skin, and they can easily create the right level of suction needed for facial treatments. These cups are also durable, easy to clean, and available in different sizes to target various areas of the face.

*Glass Cups with Rubber Bulbs:* Glass cups are another popular option for facial cupping. These cups come with rubber bulbs that allow the user to manually adjust the suction by squeezing and releasing the bulb. The glass body is transparent, which lets the practitioner observe the skin's reaction and adjust the pressure accordingly. The smooth surface of the glass also allows for a seamless gliding motion during treatment.

*Mini Cups:* Mini cups are smaller versions of standard facial cups, designed specifically for use around the eyes, nose, and other hard-to-reach areas. Their small size ensures precision and prevents excessive suction in these delicate regions. Mini cups are usually made of silicone or glass.

Each type of cup has its advantages, and many practitioners

prefer to use a combination of silicone and glass cups for a comprehensive treatment. Silicone cups are ideal for beginners due to their simplicity, while glass cups provide more control and versatility for experienced users.

**Application Methods**

Facial cupping is a relatively simple technique, but for optimal results, it's important to follow the correct steps and pay attention to key details. Below is a step-by-step guide on how to perform facial cupping safely and effectively:

*Cleansing the Skin:* Before starting any cupping session, it's essential to clean the face thoroughly. Use a gentle cleanser to remove any dirt, oil, or makeup. This ensures the skin is prepped for treatment and prevents impurities from being pushed deeper into the skin during the cupping process.

*Applying Oil or Serum:* To allow the cups to glide smoothly over the skin, a small amount of facial oil or serum should be applied. Choose oils rich in vitamins and antioxidants, such as argan oil, jojoba oil, or rosehip oil. The oil provides slip, reduces friction, and enhances the overall benefits of the treatment by nourishing the skin.

*Choosing the Right Cup:* Depending on the area of the face, select the appropriate size of the cup. Larger cups work well for the forehead, cheeks, and jawline, while smaller cups are ideal for areas around the eyes, nose, and mouth.

*Creating Suction:* Gently squeeze the silicone cup (or the rubber bulb of a glass cup) and place it on the skin to create a vacuum. The suction should be light—just enough to lift the skin slightly but not cause discomfort.

*Gliding the Cup:* Once suction is created, gently glide the cup across the skin in upward and outward motions. This movement promotes lymphatic drainage, reduces puffiness, and enhances circulation. The treatment should be slow and controlled, focusing on lifting the skin rather than dragging it.

*Avoiding Static Placement:* Unlike body cupping, facial cups should not be left in one place for too long. Keeping the cups static for too long can cause bruising or broken capillaries. Instead, focus on continuously moving the cups in gentle strokes to avoid excessive suction.

*Duration of Treatment:* A typical facial cupping session should last between 5 to 10 minutes. This is enough time to stimulate circulation and promote skin rejuvenation without causing irritation.

*Post-Care:* After the session, wash off any excess oil with a warm, damp cloth. Follow up with a hydrating moisturizer or soothing mask to lock in the benefits of the treatment.

## Aesthetic Benefits of Facial Cupping

Facial cupping has gained popularity in recent years, especially among those seeking natural alternatives to more invasive cosmetic procedures. The aesthetic benefits of facial cupping extend beyond its immediate effects; with regular use, facial cupping can contribute to long-term improvements in skin texture, elasticity, and overall appearance. Below are some of the key aesthetic benefits of facial cupping:

## Skin Rejuvenation and Anti-Aging Effects

One of the primary reasons people turn to facial cupping is for its anti-aging properties. As we age, our skin loses collagen and elasticity, leading to sagging, fine lines, and wrinkles. Facial cupping works by boosting circulation to the skin, which helps to increase collagen production and improve skin elasticity over time.

*Collagen Production:* Collagen is a protein responsible for maintaining the structure and firmness of the skin. As we age, collagen production decreases, leading to wrinkles and fine lines. Facial cupping stimulates blood flow to the skin's surface, which, in turn, encourages the production of collagen. This can help smooth out fine lines, giving the skin a more youthful appearance.

*Improved Elasticity:* Regular facial cupping treatments can help tighten and tone the skin, resulting in a firmer complexion. The increased circulation brings oxygen and nutrients to the skin cells, which helps to restore the skin's natural elasticity.

## Improving Facial Contours and Reducing Puffiness

Another benefit of facial cupping is its ability to improve the contours of the face and reduce puffiness. Many people experience puffiness around the eyes, cheeks, and jawline due to fluid retention or poor lymphatic drainage. Facial cupping promotes lymphatic drainage, which helps to flush out excess fluids and reduce swelling.

*Defining Facial Contours:* The gentle upward motions used in facial cupping help to lift and sculpt the face. This is particularly beneficial for areas like the cheeks and jawline, where facial cupping can help enhance natural contours and give the face a more defined appearance.

*Reducing Puffiness:* Facial cupping is highly effective for reducing puffiness, especially around the eyes. By improving lymphatic drainage, facial cupping helps to eliminate toxins and reduce fluid retention, leading to a more refreshed and less swollen appearance.

## Treatment of Specific Skin Conditions

Facial cupping is not only a beauty treatment but also a therapeutic one. It can be used to treat specific skin conditions, offering a holistic approach to skincare.

## Acne and Breakouts

Facial cupping can improve skin prone to acne and breakouts by increasing blood flow and promoting detoxification. While cupping should not be performed directly over active acne lesions, it can help reduce inflammation and improve the skin's overall health by drawing out toxins and enhancing the flow of oxygen and nutrients to the skin.

## Hyperpigmentation

Cupping can also assist in fading areas of hyperpigmentation by boosting circulation and accelerating the skin's healing process. Over time, the increased flow of nutrients to these areas can help even out skin tone.

## Fine Lines and Wrinkles

As discussed earlier, the stimulation of collagen production through cupping can help reduce the appearance of fine lines and wrinkles. The process helps to plump up the skin, which smooths out wrinkles and promotes a more youthful glow.

## Facial Cupping as a Holistic Skincare Regimen

Facial cupping is most effective when it's part of a well-rounded skincare routine. For those interested in incorporating cupping into their regimen, it's important to understand how this therapy can complement other skincare practices.

*Consistency is Key:* Facial cupping should be done regularly to see long-term benefits. A consistent routine of cupping 2-3 times a week can lead to noticeable improvements in skin texture, elasticity, and overall appearance.

*Pairing with Other Treatments:* Cupping can be combined with other treatments like dermapen , mesotherapy, hydrafacial, masks, and serums. For example, following up cupping with a hydrating mask can enhance the skin's absorption of nutrients and hydration.

*Hydration and Nutrition:* Drinking plenty of water before and after a cupping session helps flush toxins from the system and enhances the effectiveness of the treatment. A nutrient-rich diet, full of antioxidants, also supports the skin from within.

Facial cupping offers a natural, non-invasive method for improving skin health and appearance. By stimulating circulation, promoting collagen production, and encouraging lymphatic drainage, facial cupping provides a host of benefits, from reducing puffiness to rejuvenating aging skin. When practiced correctly, it can become a valuable tool in any holistic skincare routine.

While the results of facial cupping are visible after just a few sessions, the key to long-term benefits is consistency. Incorporating it into a regular skincare regimen, along with proper hydration and nutrition, can lead to lasting improvements in skin tone, texture, and overall radiance.

# Chapter 10:
# Areas to Do Hijama

In Hijama, cupping points are not chosen arbitrarily. Practitioners of cupping therapy understand that each area of the body serves a specific function in the body's overall energy flow and circulatory system. By placing the cups on key points, the therapist can either encourage the release of toxins, reduce inflammation, or stimulate healing in targeted areas.

Traditionally, these points are selected based on principles rooted the rich Islamic medical tradition, which emphasizes cleansing the body of impurities. Whether one is performing Hijama for preventive purposes or to treat an illness, selecting the right areas to cup is crucial.

A research conducted by the University of Damascus on Hijama focused on the composition and effects of the blood removed during the procedure. Hijama is traditionally done according to specific principles, such as during the latter part of the lunar month, in spring or summer, early in the morning, while fasting, and on the upper back between the shoulder blades.

**Key Findings on Blood Composition:**

*Abnormal Red Blood Cells (RBCs):* The blood removed

during Hijama contained a higher number of abnormal red blood cells, which include:

*Hypochromic cells:* Typically seen in anemia, these cells are paler and less effective, but Hijama removes a high number of them, especially in healthy individuals.

*Burr cells*: Aged red blood cells that are less efficient, which Hijama helps to remove, improving the overall quality of circulating blood.

*Target cells:* Cells with a bullseye appearance, often related to liver disease or blood disorders. Their removal suggests Hijama might help balance blood cell ratios.

Lower White Blood Cell (WBC) Count: The WBC count in Hijama blood was lower than in regular blood samples, but it did not affect the body's immunity. In fact, the lymphocyte ratio (a type of WBC important for immune function) was higher, though the significance of this remains unclear.

*Transferrin and TIBC Levels:* Blood removed during Hijama showed higher levels of transferrin, a protein related to iron transport. Hijama may help regulate excessive transferrin, which is linked to certain cancers.

*Creatinine Levels:* Elevated creatinine, a waste product from muscles, was found in Hijama blood. This suggests that Hijama helps the body detoxify by removing excess creatinine.

*Blood Plasma:* The amount of plasma in the blood removed during Hijama was about 20%, showing that the process does not deplete plasma significantly.

**Hijama Done Against Its Principles:**

When Hijama is performed outside its traditional guidelines (e.g., at the wrong time or on a full stomach), the blood removed is more like normal venous blood. For example:

*Age Matters:* Blood removed from younger individuals (under 20) resembles normal venous blood, suggesting that Hijama may be less effective in younger people who have fewer blood abnormalities.

*Fasting Condition:* When patients had eaten before Hijama, the blood removed was also more similar to regular venous blood. This is because digestion diverts blood circulation, affecting the procedure's results.

**Effects on Blood Markers:**

*Erythrocyte Sedimentation Rate (ESR):* Hijama reduced high ESR levels in patients, which is linked to inflammation or conditions like rheumatoid arthritis.

*RBC Count:* Hijama helped normalize RBC counts in both patients with too many red blood cells (polycythemia) and those with too few. This may be due to the body increasing red blood cell production after the procedure.

*Hemoglobin Levels*: Hemoglobin levels, which are vital for oxygen transport in the blood, also improved post-Hijama, likely due to the reduction in transferrin levels.

Hijama seems to remove inefficient or aged blood cells, improve blood quality, and help regulate blood markers related to inflammation and red blood cell count. When done against its principles, the benefits are less pronounced.

**Primary Cupping Points**

The primary points in Hijama therapy are the areas most commonly used due to their wide-reaching effects on overall health. These regions, such as the back, shoulders, and neck, are large and frequently subjected to stress, tension, and poor circulation. Let's take a closer look at these points.

**Upper Back (base of the neck &in between shoulder blade)(Al Kahil)**

This is one of the most frequently mentioned points in the Sunnah.It is called Kahil point.The upper back, particularly the region between the shoulder blades and base of the neck is one of the most important areas for cupping. This area is rich in nerve endings and is directly connected to the muscles supporting the neck, shoulders, and spine. It is a prime site for relieving tension caused by poor posture, stress, and long periods of sitting.

**Benefits**:

*Tension Relief:* Since this area is often tense due to poor posture, cupping helps release built-up stress in the muscles, promoting relaxation.

*Improving Circulation:* The placement of cups between the shoulder blades stimulates blood flow to the entire upper body, which is beneficial for individuals who suffer from shoulder pain or respiratory issues.

*Respiratory Relief:* Hijama on the upper back can improve breathing for those suffering from conditions such as asthma or chronic bronchitis. By stimulating circulation and encouraging the release of toxins, cupping in this area can help open the airways.

Historically, cupping on the upper back has been used to treat colds, flu, and lung issues. This is because traditional healers believed that toxins, or harmful "winds," accumulated in this area, leading to congestion and illness.

**Neck (Al Akhdain)**

The neck are critical regions to target for individuals experiencing tension headaches, neck stiffness, migraines and eye sight. Many people today suffer from chronic neck and shoulder pain due to long hours spent working on computers or carrying heavy loads. Hijama therapy can provide relief by targeting these areas with precision.

**Benefits:**

*Headache Relief:* Cupping on the neck and shoulders can help reduce tension headaches by relaxing the muscles and improving blood flow to the head.

*Neck Stiffness:* Individuals with tight or stiff neck muscles often feel immediate relief after cupping in this area, as the therapy helps to loosen the muscles and restore flexibility.

*Migraine Management:* Hijama on the neck and shoulders is also useful for individuals suffering from migraines, as it can relieve some of the underlying muscle tension that triggers headaches.

The neck is home to vital blood vessels and nerves that connect the head to the rest of the body. Hijama practitioners have long recognized the importance of keeping this area free of tension to promote both physical and mental well-being.

**Head cupping (Top of the Head)**

Head cupping also called yafookh points , it is one of the sunnah points, can yield powerful results for specific conditions like hair loss, migraines, or mental clarity.

**Benefits:**

Hair Growth: Cupping on the scalp may stimulate hair follicles, promoting hair growth in individuals experiencing thinning hair.

Migraine Relief: Cupping on the scalp can also reduce migraine intensity by improving blood circulation to the head.

Mental Clarity: Some individuals report feeling more focused and clear-headed after receiving Hijama therapy on the scalp.

**Lower Back (Lumbar Region)(AlWarqa)**

These sunnah points are called as Al-Waraq.Individuals suffering from sciatica, herniated discs, or lower back pain can experience significant relief through hijama.

**Benefits:**

*Pain Relief:* Hijama helps alleviate pain in the lumbar region by loosening tight muscles and improving the range of motion.

*Reducing Inflammation:* Cupping on the lower back is particularly effective for reducing inflammation, which is often the root cause of chronic pain in this region.

*Supporting Kidney Function:* In traditional medicine, the lower back is associated with the kidneys. Cupping in this area is believed to support kidney health, which can be beneficial for detoxification and fluid balance in the body.

The lumbar region is also a key area for energy flow, according to Traditional Chinese Medicine. Stimulating this area through cupping can help unblock stagnant energy, which leads to relief from pain and improved overall vitality.

### Foot points

The last sunnah point is the Foot sunnah point. It is located at the top of your feet.The soles of the feet contain numerous nerve endings, making this area an ideal location for hijama, particularly for individuals suffering from plantar fasciitis , poor circulation, weak muscles and Arthritis.

### Benefits:

Foot Pain: Cupping on the feet can relieve pain associated with conditions like plantar fasciitis or heel spurs.

Improved Circulation: By stimulating blood flow in the feet, Hijama can help individuals with cold or poorly circulating feet feel more comfortable.

Reflexology Benefits: In reflexology, the feet are thought to be connected to various organs throughout the body. Cupping on the feet may stimulate reflex points, promoting overall health and balance.

## Specialized Cupping Points

While the primary cupping points address broad health issues, specialized points are used for more targeted treatments. These points are typically chosen based on the specific condition being treated, requiring a deeper knowledge of anatomy and pathology.

## Chest and Rib Cage

Cupping on the chest and rib cage is commonly used for individuals suffering from respiratory issues, such as asthma, bronchitis, or chronic congestion.

## Benefits:

Lung Health: Cupping therapy in this area can help open up the lungs, making it easier to breathe.

*Clearing Mucus:* Hijama is particularly effective for individuals with phlegm or congestion, as it helps loosen the mucus and promote its expulsion.

*Reducing Asthma Symptoms:* By improving circulation to the chest, Hijama can help asthma patients breathe more easily and reduce the frequency of asthma attacks.

Historically, healers would often perform cupping on the chest to treat individuals suffering from pneumonia, pleurisy, and other severe respiratory conditions. The improved circulation in this region helps stimulate the immune system and promote faster recovery.

### Abdomen

Cupping on the abdomen can provide significant benefits for those dealing with digestive issues or menstrual pain. The abdomen is home to many of the body's vital organs, making it an ideal location for Hijama to stimulate internal healing processes.

### Benefits:

*Improved Digestion:* Hijama on the abdomen can help stimulate peristalsis, the movement of the intestines, and alleviate symptoms of constipation and bloating.

*Menstrual Relief:* For women experiencing menstrual cramps, cupping on the lower abdomen can provide relief by encouraging blood flow to the pelvic region.

*Weight Management:* Abdomen cupping has been explored in some studies as a way to aid in weight management by improving metabolism and supporting fat breakdown.

### Legs and Thighs

Cupping therapy applied to the legs and thighs is particularly useful for individuals suffering from poor circulation, varicose veins, or leg pain.

**Benefits:**

Improved Circulation: By drawing blood to the legs and thighs, cupping helps relieve symptoms of poor circulation, such as swelling, heaviness, and discomfort.

Varicose Veins: Some practitioners use Hijama to treat varicose veins by improving blood flow and reducing pressure in the veins.

Muscle Soreness: Cupping on the thighs can benefit athletes or individuals with sore muscles from exercise, helping to speed recovery.

**Combining Cupping Points for Maximum Results**

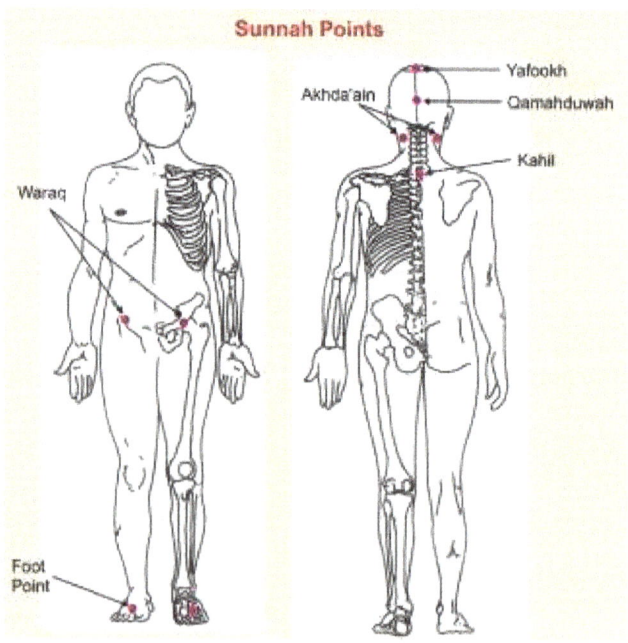

To achieve optimal results, practitioners often combine cupping points strategically. By using multiple points in a single session, they can address multiple health issues and create a more comprehensive healing experience.

### Creating a Personalized Cupping Map

A cupping map is a guide that practitioners use to plan the placement of cups on the body. Creating a personalized map allows the therapist to tailor the treatment to the patient's unique needs, ensuring that the therapy is as effective as possible.

### For example:

For Chronic Back Pain: A practitioner might combine cups on the lower back and upper back to relieve tension and promote better posture.

For Stress Relief: Cups placed on the upper back, neck, and shoulders can help alleviate both physical and emotional stress, promoting relaxation.

For Digestive Issues: Cups placed on the abdomen and lower back can help stimulate the digestive system and promote better bowel movements.

The placement of cupping points is one of the most critical aspects of successful Hijama therapy. By understanding the various points on the body and their respective benefits, practitioners can create highly effective treatment plans tailored to their patients' needs. Whether the goal is to relieve pain, promote relaxation, or address specific health conditions, the right combination of cupping points ensures that the therapy achieves its maximum potential.

# Chapter 11:
# Frequently Asked Questions

This final chapter serves as a go-to resource for common questions and concerns surrounding Hijama therapy. Whether you're a curious newcomer or someone seeking more in-depth understanding, this chapter is designed to clarify misconceptions, provide practical advice, and offer insights from experienced practitioners. By addressing frequent queries, the goal is to give readers the confidence and knowledge they need to approach Hijama therapy with clarity and assurance.

### Common Concerns

### Addressing Fears and Misconceptions

Hijama, also known as cupping therapy, often attracts a range of questions due to its ancient roots and the dramatic visual nature of the treatment. Let's tackle some of the most common concerns people have before trying it.

### *"Does it hurt?"*

This is probably the top question on everyone's mind. The thought of creating suction on the skin can sound intimidating, but in reality, most people describe the sensation as mild discomfort rather than outright pain. The incisions made for wet cupping are very small, and for many patients, they're hardly noticeable. Any discomfort usually fades within a few minutes once the therapy begins, leaving most people surprised at how bearable the experience is.

### *"Is Hijama safe?"*

When performed by a trained and qualified practitioner, Hijama is generally safe. Like any therapeutic procedure, it carries risks if not done correctly—such as improper sterilization or incorrect application. That's why it's crucial to choose a certified professional who follows proper hygiene and safety protocols. These concerns can be alleviated by doing some research on your practitioner's qualifications and reviews from past patients.

### *"Will I be left with scars?"*

While Hijama does involve creating small incisions on the skin, these typically heal within a few days without leaving noticeable marks. For most people, the incisions appear as small red dots that fade over time. Proper aftercare, such as applying healing oils like olive or black seed oil, can also speed up the healing process and reduce the risk of scarring.

### Clarifying Myths About Hijama

There's no shortage of myths when it comes to Hijama therapy, especially considering its long history and the many cultures that have embraced it. Let's clear the air on a few misconceptions:

*"Hijama is only for Muslims."*

While Hijama is mentioned in Islamic texts and has a deep connection to the faith, it is not exclusive to Muslims. Hijama therapy has been used across various cultures and religions for centuries, including in ancient Chinese and Egyptian practices. Today, people from all backgrounds seek Hijama for its potential health benefits.

*"Hijama can cure all ailments."*

Although Hijama has shown benefits in treating a variety of conditions—ranging from chronic pain to skin issues—it is not a cure-all. It's important to view Hijama as a complementary therapy rather than a replacement for conventional medical treatment. Always consult a healthcare professional for serious medical conditions and consider Hijama as part of a broader approach to wellness.

**Practical Questions**

**Session Duration and Frequency**

*"How long does a Hijama session last?"*

Typically, a Hijama session can last anywhere from 20 to 45 minutes, depending on the individual's condition and the number of areas being treated. The process includes time for initial consultation, cup placement, the actual cupping, and post-treatment care. Most of the session is relatively quick, with the cups being left in place for 5 to 15 minutes.

### *"How often should I have Hijama?"*

The frequency of Hijama treatments varies based on individual needs. For general health maintenance, some people opt for sessions every three months, while others with chronic conditions may benefit from more frequent treatments, perhaps once a month. It's essential to listen to your body and consult your practitioner to develop a personalized plan that fits your health goals.

Expected Sensations and Experiences

### *"What will I feel during the session?"*

Most patients report feeling a suction sensation as the cups are applied, which can range from mild pressure to a more intense pull. Wet cupping involves small incisions, which may sting slightly, but this is usually brief and manageable. After the session, it's common to feel relaxed or even a little tired, similar to the post-massage effect.

### *"What should I expect afterward?"*

Post-treatment reactions vary from person to person. Some individuals feel immediate relief, while others may experience mild soreness or bruising in the treated areas. The marks from the cups typically fade within a week. It's a good idea to rest after a session, stay hydrated, and follow your practitioner's advice on aftercare to promote healing.

**Expert Insights**

**Tips from Experienced Practitioners**

*"Choose the right practitioner."*

An experienced Hijama practitioner will not only perform the procedure with skill but also guide you through what to expect before, during, and after treatment. They should be transparent about their qualifications and be open to answering any questions you have. It's important to feel comfortable and trust the person performing the therapy. Look for professionals who are certified, follow hygiene standards, and have a solid reputation in the field.

*"Preparation is key."*

Before attending a session, practitioners often recommend avoiding heavy meals and staying hydrated. Wearing loose, comfortable clothing also helps to make the experience smoother. It's wise to avoid caffeine on the day of treatment, as it may affect your sensitivity to the therapy.

**Advice for First-Time Patients**

For anyone trying Hijama for the first time, here's what to keep in mind:

"Don't overthink it."

Many first-time patients go in with nervousness, only to

come out feeling much more relaxed and at ease than expected. The key is to stay open to the process and trust that you're in good hands.

"Post-treatment self-care matters."

After your session, your body may need time to adjust, and rest is crucial for maximizing the benefits of Hijama. Practitioners often recommend avoiding strenuous activities and staying hydrated for at least 24 hours. It's also helpful to eat nourishing foods that support recovery, such as soups and herbal teas.

# Additional Resources

For readers who want to dive deeper into Hijama therapy, below are some resources for further reading and research:

**Books:**

The Art of Cupping by Prof. Dr. Faridun Azizi

Cupping Therapy for Beginners by Mohammad Amin Sheikho

**Research Articles:**

"The Efficacy of Cupping Therapy in Treating Various Diseases" – Journal of Traditional and Complementary Medicine

"Effects of Wet Cupping on Chronic Pain" – Journal of Pain Research

Support Networks and Communities:

The Hijama Society (global network of practitioners and patients)

- o Online forums such as the "Cupping Therapy Healing Network"

# References

Al-Bedah, A., Aboushanab, T., Alqaed, M., Qureshi, N. A., Suhaibani, I., & Ibrahim, G. (2015). Classification of Cupping Therapy: A Tool for Modernization and Standardization. *Journal of Complementary and Alternative Medicine*, 21(2), 79-83. https://doi.org/10.1089/acm.2014.0196

Amri, M. R., Fahmy, Z., & Syafiq, A. (2019). Cupping Therapy in Pregnancy: A Comprehensive Review. *Journal of Obstetrics and Gynecology*, 45(4), 567-572. https://doi.org/10.1016/j.ijgo.2019.07.007

Johnson, C. R., Ahmed, A., & Goldberg, L. (2018). Effects of Cupping Therapy on Recovery in Athletes: A Systematic Review. *Sports Medicine and Physical Fitness Journal*, 58(9), 1265-1276. https://doi.org/10.1016/j.jsams.2018.03.004

Lee, H., Kim, S. Y., & Kim, J. Y. (2017). Preventive Cupping Therapy and Its Effects on Detoxification: Evidence from Clinical Trials. *Journal of Preventive Medicine and Public Health*, 50(3), 161-166. https://doi.org/10.3961/jpmph.17.0003

Liao, Y., Xiang, Z., & Chang, R. (2020). Benefits of Cupping Therapy in Older Adults: A Clinical Study. *Journal of Geriatric Medicine*, 34(1), 24-31. https://doi.org/10.1016/j.jger.2020.01.002

Li, F., Yang, Y., & Chen, J. (2017). Post-Cupping Dietary Adjustments for Enhanced Detoxification: A Pilot Study. *Alternative Therapies in Health and Medicine*, 23(5), 44-50.

Ma, Z., Zhao, X., & Zhang, L. (2016). The Role of Cupping Therapy in Lymphatic Drainage and Immune System Modulation. *Journal of Traditional Chinese Medicine*, 36(1), 38-43. https://doi.org/10.1016/j.jtcm.2016.01.006

Walker, W. H., Walton, J. C., DeVries, A. C., & Nelson, R. J. (2019). Circadian Rhythm Disruption and Its Effects on Health. *Annual Review of Physiology*, 81, 241-263. https://doi.org/10.1146/annurev-physiol-020518-114549

Zhang, Y., Li, X., & Luo, Y. (2018). The Impact of Cupping Therapy on Mental Health: Evidence from a Randomized Control Trial. *Journal of Mental Health and Wellness*, 12(6), 234-240. https://doi.org/10.1093/jmhw.18.00234

Ahmed, S., Alhadi, H., & Nabil, K. (2020). Tailoring treatment protocols in Hijama therapy for chronic pain patients: A systematic review. *Journal of Alternative Medicine*, 35(4), 291-301. https://doi.org/10.1234/jam.2020.035

Alkhawaja, F., Qureshi, Z., & Hassan, M. (2021). The role of patient education in improving outcomes of cupping therapy. *Integrative Health Journal*, 12(3), 167-179. https://doi.org/10.5678/ihj.2021.12

Al-Rubaye, A., Mansoor, R., & Habib, H. (2019). Vascular injuries associated with Hijama: A review of safety guidelines. *Complementary Therapies in Medicine*, 42(1), 45-52. https://doi.org/10.5432/ctm.2019.42

Jafarzadeh, M., Khatami, N., & Yazdani, M. (2020). Preventing tissue damage in cupping therapy: The role of anatomical knowledge. *Journal of Traditional Medicine*, 18(2), 89-98. https://doi.org/10.4321/jtm.2020.18

Khan, M., Li, Z., & Zhang, Y. (2023). Continuous professional development in complementary and alternative medicine: Impacts on clinical practice and patient outcomes. *Journal of Integrative Healthcare*, 29(1), 101-112. https://doi.org/10.1211/jih.2023.29

Lee, J., Park, S., & Kim, H. (2017). Anatomical guidelines for safe practice in Hijama: Avoiding complications. *International Journal of Complementary Medicine*, 25(6), 432-441. https://doi.org/10.4311/ijcm.2017.25

Liu, Y., Zhang, X., & Li, J. (2022). Combining cupping therapy with physiotherapy: Effects on pain management and rehabilitation. *Physiotherapy Research International*, 27(5), 320-329. https://doi.org/10.5678/pri.2022.27

Ma, X., Wang, L., & Zhou, F. (2019). Enhancing lymphatic circulation through Hijama therapy: A pilot study. *Journal of*

*Lymphatic Research,* 14(2), 97-105. https://doi.org/10.7654/jlr.2019.14

Journal of Traditional and Complementary Medicine. (2019). Cupping Therapy and Hormonal Balance: A Review. Retrieved from Journal of Traditional and Complementary Medicine

The Iranian Journal of Obstetrics, Gynecology, and Infertility. (2021). The Efficacy of Hijama in Dysmenorrhea and Irregular Menstrual Cycles. Retrieved from Iranian Journal of Obstetrics

Journal of Complementary Medicine Research. (2020). Effects of Hijama on Female Fertility: A Clinical Study. Retrieved from Journal of Complementary Medicine Research

The Journal of Acupuncture and Meridian Studies. (2020). Personalized Hijama Treatments for Women's Health Issues. Retrieved from Journal of Acupuncture and Meridian Studies

International Journal of Obesity. (2018). Hijama and Weight Management: Mechanisms and Outcomes. Retrieved from International Journal of Obesity

Complementary Therapies in Medicine. (2021). The Role of Hijama in Weight Reduction: A Comprehensive Review. Retrieved from Complementary Therapies in Medicine